UNDERSTANDING

How To Fight
The Good Fight
of Faith

UNDERSTANDING
How To Fight The Good Fight of Faith

Kenneth E. Hagin

Unless otherwise indicated, all Scripture quotations in this volume are from the *King James Version* of the Bible.

Fifth Printing 1994

ISBN 0-89276-510-0

In the U.S. write:
Kenneth Hagin Ministries
P.O. Box 50126
Tulsa, OK 74150-0126

In Canada write:
Kenneth Hagin Ministries
P.O. Box 335
Etobicoke (Toronto), Ontario
Canada, M9A 4X3

BOOKS BY KENNETH E. HAGIN

Following God's Plan For Your Life
The Triumphant Church
Healing Scriptures
Mountain Moving Faith
The Price Is Not Greater Than God's Grace (Mrs. Oretha Hagin)

MINIBOOKS (A partial listing)

* * *The New Birth*
* * *Why Tongues?*
* * *In Him*
* * *God's Medicine*
* * *You Can Have What You Say*
* *How To Write Your Own Ticket With God*
* * *Don't Blame God*
* * *Words*
* *Plead Your Case*
* * *How To Keep Your Healing*
* *The Bible Way To Receive the Holy Spirit*
* *I Went to Hell*
* *How To Walk in Love*
* *The Precious Blood of Jesus*
* * *Love Never Fails*
* *Your Faith in God Will Work*

BOOKS BY KENNETH HAGIN JR.

* * *Man's Impossibility — God's Possibility*
* *Because of Jesus*
* *How To Make the Dream God Gave You Come True*
* *The Life of Obedience*
* *God's Irresistible Word*
* *Healing: Forever Settled*
* *Don't Quit! Your Faith Will See You Through*
* *The Untapped Power in Praise*
* *Listen to Your Heart*
* *What Comes After Faith?*
* *Speak to Your Mountain!*
* *Come Out of the Valley!*

MINIBOOKS (A partial listing)

* * *Faith Worketh by Love*
* *Blueprint for Building Strong Faith*
* * *Seven Hindrances to Healing*
* * *The Past Tense of God's Word*
* *Faith Takes Back What the Devil's Stolen*
* *"The Prison Door Is Open — What Are You Still Doing Inside?"*
* *How To Be a Success in Life*
* *Get Acquainted With God*
* *Showdown With the Devil*
* *Unforgiveness*
* *Ministering to the Brokenhearted*

*These titles are also available in Spanish. Information about other foreign translations of several of the above titles (i.e., Finnish, French, German, Indonesian, Polish, Russian, etc.) may be obtained by writing to: Kenneth Hagin Ministries, P.O. Box 50126, Tulsa, Oklahoma 74150-0126.

Contents

Contents

Preface

The Body of Christ can greatly benefit by understanding who they are in Christ. Christians have suffered lack when all that God has — is already provided for us in Christ! What most believers are praying for is already theirs if they only knew how to appropriate it.

If Satan can hold us in the arena of *reason* in our minds, he can defeat us every time. But if we hold him in the arena of *faith* — we will defeat him every time! This is why it is crucial for the Christian to know what fight he is supposed to be in! The only fight the Christian is called upon to fight is *the good fight of faith.* We as Christians must understand how to fight that fight. And God has provided a full arsenal to enable His people to successfully defeat the enemy!

Kenneth E. Hagin

Tulsa, Oklahoma
May 1987

Chapter 1
Understanding the New Birth

Fight the good fight of faith. . . .
— 1 Timothy 6:12

The fight of faith is the only one the Christian is called upon to fight. I think some people have read that verse, all right, but they only read that first word "fight." They stopped right there and started fighting! Some thought it just said to fight; others thought it said, "Fight fellow Christians." They should have read the whole verse and found out what fight it was they were supposed to fight. The Bible tells us exactly what fight it is we've got to get in on: It's the good fight of faith! The faith fight is the only fight we're supposed to be in. If we're in any other fight — we're in the wrong fight.

There wouldn't be such a fight to faith, if there weren't enemies or hindrances to faith. (You can't very well have a fight without having an enemy or an opponent.)

One of the greatest enemies to faith, is the lack of understanding of the New Birth. And, you see, you cannot believe beyond your actual knowledge of God's Word. This is the reason many people fail in their prayer life and in their faith life because they are trying to believe beyond their knowledge of God's Word.

One reason we, as Christians, live in unbelief and our faith has been hindered, is because we lack knowledge about redemption and about our redemptive *rights*. We lack knowledge of what God's Word says about our redemption, and that lack of knowledge is the greatest enemy of faith. Lack of knowledge of God's Word produces unbelief. Because we don't understand what the New Birth actually is — what it means and the benefits it provides

1

the believer — our faith is hindered.

> **2 CORINTHIANS 5:17**
> 17 Therefore if any man be in Christ, he is a new creature: old things are passed away; behold, all things are become new.

Second Corinthians 5:17 is a tremendous verse of Scripture. What tremendous truths are contained in it: "... *if any man be in Christ, he is a new creature....*" The margin of the *King James Version* reads, "a new creation." Praise God, I'm glad I am a new creature — a new creation!

We Are Spirit Beings

We must realize this New Birth is speaking of the inward man — the real man — not speaking of the outward man. Remember, Paul said "... *though our outward man perish, yet the inward man is renewed day by day*" (2 Cor. 4:16). The inward man is the real you.

No one can ever know himself, much less anyone else, unless he has been born again and has become a new man in Christ. Without the New Birth man does not even know he is a spirit man.

In our modern day, many people go to a psychiatrist for someone to "understand" them. But a psychiatrist, unless he is a Christian psychiatrist, can never understand you, because only a Christian would realize that man is a spirit being. Psychiatry has to do with the operation of the mind and emotions through the physical senses. Psychiatry operates on the assumption that man is just a body and a mind (or soul).

Several years ago, I read on the front page of a

metropolitan newspaper in California that one of the leading psychiatrists in the area had committed suicide. He was a comparatively young man, only 46. Some of the leading Hollywood movie stars had been under his care.

No one could understand why this man, who seemingly had everything, would commit suicide. He lived in a beautiful, palatial home that was completely paid for. He had a large bank account and no financial troubles. He had no domestic troubles. He had no physical troubles. After the last article was run, they still didn't know why he did it. Here was a man who was supposed to help others, but evidently he didn't have the answer even for himself.

The trouble with many people is, they are always looking at things from the physical or natural viewpoint rather than from the spiritual viewpoint.

The answer to man's need exists in the spiritual realm. A man doesn't really know or understand himself unless he is a Christian, and *a man who isn't a Christian is liable to do or think anything*. This is because the spiritual nature of man is a fallen nature, and man cannot change his own nature. The Bible says, *"Can the Ethiopian change his skin, or the leopard his spots?"* (Jer. 13:23). No, man cannot change his own nature — but God can!

"Therefore if any man be in Christ, he is a new creature"! The inward man — the real man — is a new creation. This new creation takes on the very life and nature of God.

The outward man, however, is not a new creation. We do not receive new *bodies* when we are born again. The Bible says we will have a new body one day, but we don't have one yet. Meanwhile, however, the man on the inside — the real you, the spirit man — has already become a new man in Christ.

Understanding Increases Faith

I got ahold of Second Corinthians 5:17 many years ago on the bed of sickness. At that time, medical science said I could not live due to my physical condition.

I had heard salvation and the New Birth preached all my life. Although I had joined a church, I had never really been born again. Yet when I prayed to receive salvation as a bedfast teenager, I had no doubt in my mind that the Lord heard me. I had no lack of understanding along that line; therefore, I had no unbelief. I received salvation, and I knew I was saved or born again.

But there I was — still bedfast. I certainly didn't understand God's Word concerning healing for my body. We hadn't had much teaching along that line in my church. About all we had heard was, "Just leave it to the Lord. After all, He knows best."

(But in His Word, God has made provision for us to *have* His best. Praise God, He has told us how to get the best — but now it is up to us to receive what God has already provided.)

You can see how a lack of knowledge of God's Word and of our provisions in Christ can hinder faith. It hindered my faith. It kept me bedfast for 16 long months. In time, after much study of the Word, I saw the exact steps to take in prayer and just how to release my faith in order to receive healing. If I had known and understood that months before, I could have been off that bed long before I was.

God didn't have a certain "set time" to come by and

heal me. It wasn't at that "set time" that the paralysis would disappear, the incurable blood disease would leave, and the deformed heart would become normal. Because God is the same *every day!*

The trouble wasn't with God; the trouble was with me. It was my lack of knowledge of God's Word which hindered my faith. As soon as I found out what God's Word said and acted on it, I got results! We cannot act upon God's Word beyond our knowledge of His Word. *Faith grows with understanding God's Word.* If your faith is not growing, your knowledge of God's Word is not growing. If my faith were not growing, I would begin to ask myself why. Then I would begin to feed my faith on God's Word. If you are not growing in faith, you are not developing spiritually.

My understanding of Second Corinthians 5:17 made this Scripture one of my favorite verses. When I came off that bed of sickness, I told everyone I met, "I am a new creature!"

I was only 17 then and had no other Christians to fellowship with who believed as I did. I didn't have even one person, young or old, to stand with me to encourage me in this area of faith and believing God. I simply had to stand alone — but I tell you, I had a great time doing it! I am sure the one reason I didn't have some of the problems others had with the world, the flesh, or the devil was because I told everyone, "I am a new creature." That was my constant confession.

Hold fast to your confession that you are a new creature. *You will always rise to the level of your confession.* Then the new man on the inside will be manifested on the outside because he will dominate the flesh.

The Story of a New Creature

I had been raised up from the bed of sickness on the second Tuesday of August 1934. The following Saturday, the second Saturday in August 1934, I walked into town. It was a little town, then, with a population of about 9,000 people. In those days, everyone came to town on Saturday, including the surrounding farming community. All the businesses were located near the courthouse square, so on Saturdays the town was always crowded with people.

I ran into a friend of mine. Before I had become bedfast, we were bosom pals. But during the 16 months I had been bedfast, he had been to see me only once.

This Saturday he seemed really glad to see me. We sat down on the running board of a 1934 V8 Ford and began to talk about things we used to do before I became a new creature. *He* was the same old creature he had always been, but *I* had become a new creature.

From the natural standpoint, everybody has some kind of talent, although some people do not recognize that they do. These talents are just something we are born with, I suppose. I had two talents: I could always tame wild animals, and I could open any lock.

I can't tell you why, but locks intrigued me. In my early teens I could get into just about any place I wanted. And this boy was reminding me about the time I had opened the lock on some buildings and a group of boys, about 12 or 13 years of age, had gone inside.

I don't want to leave the impression that I made a practice of it, but once or twice I had managed to open a lock or two for these boys. I wouldn't go in myself, because for one thing, I was afraid of the dark. They didn't keep the stores lit up like they do now. The boys had gone inside and gotten candy. That's all they ever took, just candy. Of course, I *did* help them eat it.

My friend pointed to a building about half a block away and said, laughing, "Remember that night?"

I sat there with a mask-like look on my face and acted like I didn't know what he was talking about. (I knew what he was talking about, all right, but I was going to use this as an opportunity to witness to him.)

He finally said, "What is the matter with you?"

"Not a thing. Not a thing in the world."

"Well, you act like you don't even know what I'm talking about, and if it hadn't been for you, we couldn't have even gotten that candy." He went on talking about that night, going into more detail, and I just sat there with a blank look on my face.

"What's the matter with you?" he asked again.

"Not a thing," I replied.

"You act like you don't know what I'm talking about, and you were the one who opened that lock for us."

I said, "Lefty, the fellow who was with you boys that night is dead."

"You're not dead!" he exclaimed. "You know you're not dead."

(You see, he was looking at it from the physical standpoint. I didn't die physically. But I was looking at it from the spiritual standpoint.)

He said, "I know you *almost* died, but you're not dead. That's you sitting right there."

"Oh," I said, "you're just looking at the house I am living in. You're looking at the outward man, at the body.

The man on the inside is a new creature now in Christ Jesus."

I went on, "The Bible says in Second Corinthians 5:17 that if any man be in Christ, he is a new creature. Old things have passed away and all things have become new."

Notice what that says. *Old* things have passed away. So I was right when I told him that the old man on the inside had passed away! *All* things have become new!

Contending With the Flesh

In a new creation, of course, all things would become new. As Christians, we need to learn to let this new man — this new creation — on the inside *dominate* the outward man. The outward man is not a new man, because the body has not been born again. The body will keep on wanting to do things it used to do — things that are wrong. Paul said his body did; so don't be surprised when your body does.

1 CORINTHIANS 9:27
27 But I keep under my body, and bring it into subjection: lest that by any means, when I have preached to others, I myself should be a castaway.

Notice Paul said, *"But I keep under my body...."* Who is the "I" in that sentence?

The "I" is this man on the inside — the new man that is made new in Christ.

"... *I keep under my body* ... [I] *bring it into subjection...,"* Paul wrote.

If the body were the real you, Paul would have said, "I bring myself into subjection." But he didn't say that.

He said, "I bring *it* (he calls his body 'it') into subjection."

Into subjection to what? To the inward man.

Notice the terminology: "*I* bring my body into subjection. *I* keep under my body," or as we would say, "I keep my body under." God is not going to do something with your body. *You* are going to have to do something with your own body, or else nothing is going to be done with it. God does something with your spirit. He makes the inward man, man's spirit, a new creature. Then He sends His Holy Spirit to dwell in your spirit to give you the power so *you* can do something with the outward man.

Some people say, "Well, I can't help the things I do. I just can't help it." Yes, you can!

Paul said, "I keep my body under, and *I* bring *it* into subjection." You know as well as I do that this great man of God, this Apostle, this holy man of God, wouldn't have had to keep his body under if his body were not wanting to do things that were wrong, would he? Certainly he wouldn't!

After we are born again, we still have the flesh to contend with, and the devil will work through the flesh. In times of tests, trials, and temptations the devil will sometimes tell Christians, "You must not even be saved. If you were saved, you wouldn't want to do wrong." Satan insinuates that it was really *you* who wanted to do the wrong deed. But the man on the inside doesn't want to do wrong to begin with.

Paul's body evidently wanted to do some things that were wrong, or he wouldn't have had to keep it under subjection. He simply said, "I am not going to let my body dominate me. I bring my body into subjection. I keep it under lest by any means, after I have preached to others,

I myself should be castaway." A marginal note reads, "Lest I should be disapproved." I don't want to be disapproved by God, do you?

Remission and Forgiveness

How can a lack of knowledge in this area of the New Birth hinder faith?

Many people have told me, "Brother Hagin, before I was saved, I lived such an awful life." They go on to say they can't believe the Lord will do anything for them (such as heal their bodies or answer their prayers) because they lived such a sinful life before they were saved. These people have a lack of understanding concerning the New Birth and the "new creature" they have become in Christ.

The Word says, *"Therefore if any man be in Christ, he is a new creature"!* Old things are gone! All things become new!

When the sinner comes to Jesus, his sins are *remitted.* His sins are simply blotted out. All that he was spiritually speaking in the sight of God before he was born again is blotted out. He became a new man in Christ Jesus. God does not see anything in his life before the moment he was born again. The sinner receives *remission* of sins.

After being born again and becoming a child of God, the Christian receives *forgiveness* of sins. Remission deals with the blotting out of everything in the past — both good and bad. That is what the sinner needs. But a Christian only needs for individual sins to be taken care of which is done through receiving forgiveness of sins. (For further study in this area, *see* my minibook, *Three Big Words.)*

Peter said, *"As newborn babes, desire the sincere milk*

of the word, that ye may grow thereby" (1 Peter 2:2). He is writing to born-again Christians who have become new men and women in Christ Jesus. The Bible teaches there is a similarity between spiritual growth and physical growth. No one is born a full-grown human. We are born babies in the natural and we grow up. No one is born a full-grown Christian either. Christians are born as babies and they grow up.

Looking at a newborn babe in the natural, lying in his mother's arms, the outstanding characteristic of that baby is innocence. You hear people say, "You sweet, little innocent thing." You don't think of that baby as having a past, do you? You don't look at that little baby and say, "I wonder what awful sin he has committed?" That baby is newborn and doesn't have any past.

Now do you see what God is saying? God is saying to people who are born-again babes in Christ, "As newborn babes desire the sincere milk of the Word. You have become a new creature! You are like that newborn babe. You have no past. Your past is all gone! I am not remembering anything against you."

> ISAIAH 43:25
> 25 I, even I, am he that blotteth out thy transgressions for mine own sake, and will not remember thy sins.

> HEBREWS 8:12
> 12 ... their sins and their iniquities will I remember no more.

As He looks at you, God doesn't remember that you have any past. Why should you remember it? Remembering past sins and mistakes will hinder your faith.

Indignant Christians

I have seen people with very shady pasts be saved and filled with the Holy Spirit, or if they were backslidden, come back into fellowship with God. Sometimes Christians who had been saved awhile almost got angry about it. "I just don't understand it," they said. "That just couldn't be God. Why, God wouldn't fill a person like that with the Holy Spirit!"

I remember an incident like this when I was preaching in a certain state quite far from our home. The pastor was an old friend from Oklahoma, and he had invited us to stay in the parsonage during my meetings.

On Tuesday night I preached about the laying on of hands, then at the end of the service I laid hands on people to be healed or filled with the Spirit. I came to a certain woman in the line, and in my spirit I had a revelation about her. I had never seen her before; I had never preached in that church and didn't know anyone except the pastor. But God reveals things sometimes through the Holy Spirit, and He told me that when I laid hands on this woman, she would be filled with the Holy Spirit and would speak with other tongues.

But I also had the revelation that unless I stopped to teach a little and explain some things to this congregation before I laid my hands on her, these people would be ready to close the meeting on me. They thought a woman like her could never be baptized in the Holy Spirit, so they would declare me to be a false prophet.

I stopped right there in the prayer line and addressed the crowd. "People, this is going to surprise you. I know you don't know me. This is only the third day I have been here, so no one has told me anything about this woman. I am about to lay hands on her, and she will be filled with the Holy Spirit and speak with other tongues the minute I touch her."

I could hear gasps all over the auditorium.

I said, "The reason I am stopping to explain this is because you know she hasn't lived a very good life. I won't go into detail, but you know that and she knows that."

"I certainly do," she said.

"Ever since she was born again," I continued, "she has been in and out (more out than in) and up and down (more down than up). She has lived such a haphazard life that no one has any confidence in her or in her Christian experience."

I said to her, "Sister, I don't want to embarrass you, but that is the truth, isn't it?"

She said, "Brother Hagin, it is all true."

Then I went on. "Some people in this congregation will say, 'Well now, some of us have been seeking the baptism of the Holy Spirit for years, and if God is going to baptize anyone with the Holy Spirit, it should be us goody-goody folk.'"

Some people are so proud they are holy and humble, that they'll have to repent before they will get anything from God! It is fine to be holy, and it is fine to be spiritual, but it's wrong to be proud of it. The Bible says, *"Pride goeth before destruction ..."* (Prov. 16:18). Besides, everything we have — we got from the Lord anyway.

"What you don't know is that right in the middle of my sermon about laying on of hands to be filled with the Holy Spirit, this woman said to the Lord, 'Lord, I want to be filled with the Spirit.' She bowed her head over on the seat in front of her and — although I didn't see her do it, I have the revelation in my heart that she did it — she said, 'God, forgive me of all my sins. I have failed. I have been so weak. I have been a failure. Forgive me.' — and He did!"

I addressed her, "Sister, did you or did you not do that?"

With tears in her eyes she answered, "Brother Hagin, I did. I bowed my head over on that seat and the lady sitting beside me will tell you I did. I prayed, 'O God, I have missed it. I have been such a failure. I have been so weak. Please forgive me.' "

"Now," I said, "I want to ask this congregation something. How long do you think it will take God to forgive her? Do you suppose He has done it yet, or do you suppose He will do it sometime within the next ten years?

"The Bible says in First John 1:9, '*If we confess our sins, he is faithful and just to forgive us our sins, and to cleanse us from all unrighteousness.*' So how long did it take God to forgive and cleanse her?"

That put them on the spot.

Some of them said, "Right then."

"All right, if she is forgiven, then God will fill her right now."

I laid my hands on her and she started speaking in other tongues instantly.

In the parsonage after the service, the pastor said, "I sure am glad you stopped and explained that to the crowd. I know you don't know that woman, but we live here, and if you had just laid hands on her without an explanation, I probably would have had to close this meeting. The people would have sworn you were a false prophet."

One Woman's Hindrance

Another time after a morning teaching service in Texas,
a woman came up to talk to the pastor and me.

She said, "I want you to pray for me. My eyes have
been opened to something I never saw before. I see now
that the baptism of the Holy Spirit with the evidence of
speaking with other tongues is for us today, and I want
to be filled with the Spirit. Please pray for me."

"Well," the pastor said, "there will never be a better
time than right now."

"Oh, no, no," she said, "I couldn't be filled this morning."

"Why not?" he asked.

"I'm not quite ready yet. I'm not good enough. I have
a little more digging to do."

John Osteen, who was then a Baptist evangelist, was
standing close by, and he asked if he might say a word.
The woman was a member of a Baptist church he had
formerly pastored.

He addressed her, "Do you remember me, Sister?"

"Yes, of course. You were my pastor for several years.
In fact, it was reading your testimony about being filled
with the Holy Spirit which caused me to start attending
Full Gospel meetings. And now, since coming here, I see
the truth of it. It has been fully revealed to me," she said.

"Well, like this brother said, there will never be a better time than now," Brother Osteen stated.

"Well, yes. But I have a little more digging to do first.
I'm not quite good enough yet."

Brother Osteen smiled and said, "May I ask you a question? Have you really been born again? Do you really know

Jesus as your personal Savior?"

"Oh, yes, Brother Osteen, I know the Lord as my personal Savior. I have been born again."

"Well, fine. Do you believe the blood of the Lord Jesus Christ has cleansed you from all sin?" he asked.

"Oh, yes. Yes."

"Now, I want to ask you one more question. If you were to die — well, suppose you had a heart attack right now and fell dead here in the church — where would you go?"

"Why, I would go to heaven, of course."

"Well," he said, "if you are good enough to go to heaven right now, you ought to be good enough to get a little more of heaven in you! It is the blood of Jesus that cleanses you."

(In other words, he was saying, "You are a new creature in Christ. Recognize and enjoy the privileges of that fact.")

It dawned on that woman. She said, "Yes, that's right. I don't have any more digging to do, do I? The blood has cleansed me. I'm clean by the blood of Jesus. You just lay your hands on me and I will be filled right now."

We all reached forth our hands, but we had barely touched her when she threw up both hands and started talking in tongues. You can see how understanding the principles of God's Word helped her faith. Just a moment before there had been a hindrance. But the moment she understood the Word, faith came forth. She understood: "I am a new creature in Christ Jesus. I have been born again. I am blood washed. It's not what I did that got me ready. It's what God did for me that makes me ready."

Religious Labels

The Lord has taught me something else. We sometimes let ourselves be religiously brainwashed by whatever religious or church group we are with. Bless our hearts, we're all that way.

It was the same in New Testament days. After the Church was instituted and the Gentiles were saved, some of the brethren of the circumcision wanted the Gentiles to be circumcised. Here the Gentiles were, already saved, already baptized in the Holy Spirit, already speaking with other tongues, and these Jewish brethren said, "You cannot be saved unless you are circumcised."

A man came up to me recently and asked, "Have you ever been baptized in the Name of Jesus only?"

"No," I answered.

"Well then, you're not saved."

I laughed right outloud! "That's the funniest thing I ever heard in my life," I said.

I told him, "I have been saved and baptized in the Holy Spirit for years. Being baptized in water in anyone's *name* has nothing in the world to do with being *saved*. The New Birth is a spiritual birth; you are not born again of the water. Being born of *water* would not be a spiritual birth; being born again by the Spirit of God is a spiritual birth."

Another man came along and said to me, "I could believe you were saved if you belonged to our church."

I said, "You're the only bunch that's saved, I guess."

"That's right."

I laughed. "I've been saved for years. I'm not in your

group and not about to be!"

You can put any kind of a label on an empty can, and the can would still be empty! Just because you put a label on an empty can doesn't put anything in the can. It's not the name on the church door, or even being a member of a church that saves you. It's getting something on the inside of you — Jesus — that saves you!

I once ran into a woman who was distraught over something she'd heard preached on the radio. She said, "Well, the way that man preached, maybe I'm not even saved! Maybe no one is saved but him and his group."

I'm glad God's Kingdom is bigger than that! Praise God!

I said to her, "I just want to ask you one question: Do you think you are saved?"

"Yes, I do."

"Forget it, then," I said. "You know it. That's what counts — not what someone else says. God's Word says, *'We know that we have passed from death unto life, because we love the brethren . . .'* (1 John 3:14). I would much rather have Bible evidence that I'm saved than some man's opinion."

Not knowing the truth of the New Birth will hinder your faith and keep you from receiving the blessings God intended you to have. Walk in line with what God's Word says. Feed your faith on God's Word — and watch your faith grow!

Chapter 2
Understanding Our Place in Him

Fight the good fight of faith....
                                    — 1 Timothy 6:12

If there is a "fight" to faith, then there are enemies to faith or hindrances to faith. We are looking at vital subjects where a lack of understanding can hinder your faith.

> **ROMANS 10:17**
> **17 So then faith cometh by hearing, and hearing by the word of God.**

A lack of knowledge of God's Word is the greatest hindrance to faith. Naturally, if faith comes by hearing the Word of God as Romans 10:17 says, then it follows that a lack of hearing and understanding God's Word — produces a lack of faith.

We sometimes hear Christians praying for faith. Actually, they are not dealing with the problem correctly, because faith comes by hearing, and hearing by the Word of God. In order to receive faith it is knowledge that we need — a knowledge of the Word of God. If we receive knowledge of God's Word, we will have faith. And if we don't receive knowledge of God's Word, we won't ever have faith, because *"faith cometh by hearing, and hearing by the Word of God."* Our faith grows as our understanding of the Word of God grows.

Reviewing the New Birth

We have already seen how a lack of understanding of what the New Birth means, hinders faith. Here is what

19

God's Word says about it:

> **2 CORINTHIANS 5:17**
> 17 Therefore if any man be in Christ, he is a new creature:
> old things are passed away; behold, all things are become
> new.

In the first Chapter, "Understanding the New Birth,"
we gave instances of many people who lacked faith to
receive healing or other provisions, because they thought
since they had lived such a terrible life before they were
saved, the provisions of God were not available to them.
But the Word of God teaches that we are made new
creatures in Christ Jesus and that old things have passed
away. So when the sinner is born again and is made a new
creature in Christ, God looks upon him as though he had
never done anything wrong. The sinner, therefore, actually
receives *remission* of sins. As God said:

> **ISAIAH 43:25**
> 25 I, even I, am he that blotteth out thy transgressions
> for mine own sake, and will not remember thy sins.

With God, not only is the sinner's past remitted, but
all he was before he was saved is gone — blotted out. In
God's sight he is a new creature. That is how the believer
needs to look at it too.

As I drove along one Sunday night after a service, I
heard a radio broadcast. The speaker, who was the pastor
of a Chicago church, used this illustration in his message:

This pastor said his church maintained a mission on
"skid row," and that it took several thousand dollars a
year out of their budget to maintain it. Because some in
his congregation couldn't see the necessity of spending

this money, one Sunday night this pastor brought in one man who had been gloriously born again in that mission. The pastor wanted his congregation to see an example of the wonderful things that were happening as a result of this mission.

The gentleman the pastor brought in explained that he had been saved only three years before. In his testimony, this man related that he had been educated as a lawyer and that at 30 years of age he had owned a fine home, and had driven the finest of automobiles. But he began to drink a little bit socially. At first he was certain he could handle it. Yet he kept drinking more and more until it was apparent he was an alcoholic.

Finally, he wasn't able to carry on his business anymore. His law partners became disgusted with him and disassociated themselves from him. His wife couldn't live with him anymore and she left, taking their only child, a 12-year-old daughter.

At 34 years of age this man had lost everything. He spent the next 30 years of his life as a destitute alcoholic.

Then at 64, in this mission, he went to the altar and received salvation. God instantly delivered him from alcoholism. Since then he had lived and worked at the mission where he had been instrumental in leading other alcoholics to the Lord.

The pastor said to him, "I want you to go into a little detail about some things that have happened in your life; how you have lived these 30 years. Go into some of the sordid areas of that life — as far as you can in a mixed congregation."

He did go into detail on a few things which shocked the people. But with tears he said, "I'm not telling this because I'm proud of it, because I am not. I am merely saying this to show you how God can deliver a person, no matter how deeply into sin he may have gone."

In relating this story on the broadcast, the pastor said that in the service that night there was a 13-year-old girl sitting on the front pew. Her mother and father were Christians, but this girl had never made any commitment to Christ.

The pastor related that the 67-year-old gentleman suddenly stopped in his testimony and pointed to this girl, saying, "I regret all of this. I would give anything in the world if I were as clean as this young girl is." The pastor spoke up and said, "You are *cleaner* if she has never been born again."

Did you ever stop to think about that? He spoke a truth. You see, we look at things from the natural standpoint. But God looks at things from the spiritual standpoint. And in the sight of God, spiritual sins are worse than physical sins!

We, however, cannot see spiritual sins. We see people do things outwardly and we say, "That's terrible." And it may well be, yet people can have things on the inside of them that are far worse in the sight of God.

For example, as Christians we know that things such as practicing witchcraft are wrong and of the devil. We know that evil spirits are involved in such practices. And the Bible says, *"For rebellion is as the sin of witchcraft . . ."* (1 Sam. 15:23). But even Christians rebel sometimes. They rebel against God's plan and against God's Word. Well, we can't see rebellion, but the Bible says it is as witchcraft.

When I pastored, there was a certain man in the con-

gregation who was used mightily in spiritual manifestations. That is, the gifts of the Spirit were manifested
through him and some great things happened in the services. But I had seen something in him that I didn't think
was too Christlike.

I said to the Lord, "Now, Lord, I don't know how many
other people can see this about that man, but why couldn't
you have used Sister So-and-so instead of him?" (And I
mentioned a dear old saint, a lady who had been in the
congregation many years and whom everyone considered
to be a real saint of God.) "It looks to me like the
manifestations of the Spirit should have come through
her." I continued, "Some people would have had more confidence in these spiritual manifestations if they had,
because she is such a stalwart, separated, dedicated
Christian."

The Lord said to me, "I don't look on the outward
appearance. You saw something on the outside of that man
which was not right. But there's something you don't
know. The very minute he saw he had gotten into this particular area, he said, 'Dear God, I have missed it. I have
failed You. Forgive me and cleanse me.' I did and he is
walking with Me.

"You also don't know this: That woman has been
rebellious in her spirit for more than 40 years. I see that
rebellion. It comes up before me dark and black, mean and
ugly. Outside she is as those Jesus spoke to, saying, '*Woe
unto you, scribes and Pharisees, hypocrites! for ye are like
unto whited sepulchres, which indeed appear beautiful outward, but are within full of dead men's bones, and of all
uncleanness'* " (Matt. 23:27).

That is why the Bible says, "*Judge not, that ye be not*

judged" (Matt. 7:1). We humans cannot judge righteous judgment.

The pastor understood this, so he said to the redeemed alcoholic, "In the sight of God you are cleaner, purer, and more innocent than this young girl if she's never been born again." This pastor also understood that, *". . . if any man be in Christ, he is a new creature: old things are passed away; behold, all things are become new."* Notice *". . . all things are become new."* That means there are no sin scars left on the Christian. (I didn't say there may not be sin scars left on the body — but the body is not the real you.)

> **1 CORINTHIANS 9:27**
> 27 But I keep under my body, and bring it into subjection:
> lest that by any means, when I have preached to others,
> I myself should be a castaway.

Paul said, *"I keep under my body, and bring IT into subjection. . . ."* He calls his body "it." The body is merely the house you live in. Because of sins of the past, there may be sin scars left on your body, but there are no sin scars left on *you.*

God looks at that new man in Christ when He looks at you. And you know, we look a lot better in Christ than we do out of Him. We may not be able to see each other in Christ, but God can. We look at each other from the natural standpoint, but God looks at us in Him!

Our Place in Him — His Place in Us

A lack of understanding of our place in Him and His place in our lives hinders us from success and throttles faith. It is the reason for unbelief in our Christian walk.

People often ask me about how to study the Bible. Although I have many suggestions, there is one above all others I present everywhere I go. As a believer and as a Christian, may I suggest you follow this method as you go through the New Testament, primarily the Epistles. You see, the Epistles are the letters written to you, the believer.

No one could ever be a successful Christian and live only in the four Gospels. If you only read and lived in the four Gospels, you wouldn't even know why Jesus died. You might think you would (because you had already read the Epistles), but just by reading the Gospels do you think you'd know more than the apostles did? They were with Jesus every day for more than three years, yet they didn't know why He died. They asked Him, *"Lord, wilt thou at this time restore again the kingdom to Israel?"* (Acts 1:6).

Remember how John wrote that he and Peter ran to the tomb after Mary told them Jesus was not there? John, being the smaller of the two, outran Peter, who was a bigger, more lumbering type. But John, with his finer, more sensitive nature (because the dead and the tombs were very sacred to the Jews), didn't go inside Jesus' tomb. He stopped outside of it. Peter, being impulsive, ducked his head and went right on in through the opening of the tomb. Then John followed him.

John writes, *"Then went in also that other disciple, which came first to the sepulchre, and he saw, and believed. For as yet they knew not the scripture, that he must rise again from the dead"* (John 20:8,9). The disciples themselves didn't know why Jesus died!

However, the thing that convinced the disciples of Jesus' resurrection was this: According to John 19:39-42,

Jesus was embalmed after the manner of the Jews.

JOHN 19:39-42
39 And there came also Nicodemus, which at the first came to Jesus by night, and brought a mixture of myrrh and aloes, about an hundred pound weight.
40 Then took they the body of Jesus, and wound it in linen clothes with the spices, as the manner of the Jews is to bury.
41 Now in the place where he was crucified there was a garden; and in the garden a new sepulchre, wherein was never man yet laid.
42 There laid they Jesus therefore because of the Jews' preparation day; for the sepulchre was nigh at hand.

The Jews had learned embalming from the Egyptians when they were in captivity in Egypt those 430 years. The Egyptians made a sticky tar-like substance from the mixture of myrrh and aloes. Then thin strips of cloth were smeared with this substance and the body was wrapped in these strips of cloth. This made a sort of cocoon around the corpse. Each toe and finger was individually wrapped.

One reason Mary was going to the tomb on the first day of the week after the Jewish Sabbath, was to finish the embalming. The face had not yet been finished. They had left that part of the cocoon open and had laid a napkin over it.

From all historical evidence, Jesus was about 5 feet 11 and probably weighed about 180 pounds. In that warm country, He probably would have shrunk in His death, decreasing His body weight by about 20 pounds. The hundred pounds of myrrh and aloes, and the grave clothes, probably weighed about 120 pounds. So with the body, the myrrh and aloes, and the grave clothes, that cocoon probably would have weighed about 280 pounds.

Jesus came out of the face opening and left the cocoon lying there. The napkin which had covered the face was folded — it wasn't just flung to one side. When Peter and John saw this, they were convinced no one had carried Him away. How could anyone get Him out of that sort of thing?

You can see that by reading the four Gospels, a person wouldn't really be able to grasp why Jesus died. The Gospels have to do with His life, death, burial, and resurrection. But it is in the letters — the Epistles — written to the Church where the Bible tells us exactly *why* Jesus died. It is in the Epistles where you find out what happened to Jesus the moment He died, where He went, and what He did.

It is also in the Epistles where Paul wrote, "... *the gospel which was preached of me is not after man. For I neither received it of man, neither was I taught it, but by the revelation of Jesus Christ*" (Gal. 1:11,12).

Furthermore, you find out in the Epistles what happened to Jesus *after* He was raised from the dead. Mary, you remember, saw Jesus at the tomb and He said to her, "... *Touch me not*..." (John 20:17). Yet when He appeared to the disciples (who were frightened, supposing they were seeing a ghost), He said, "... *handle me, and see; for a spirit hath not flesh and bones, as ye see me have*" (Luke 24:39).

Why would Jesus say to Mary, the first person He saw, "Don't touch me" and then a short time later say to the disciples, "Handle me, touch me, so you can see I am flesh and bone"?

This question is answered in the Epistles, for it is in the Epistles where we see what really happened between the time Jesus told Mary, "*Touch me not; for I am not*

yet ascended to my Father ..." (John 20:17), and His
second appearance later to the disciples. The Bible tells
us in the Book of Hebrews that between those two
appearances, Jesus entered into the heavenly Holy Place
with His own blood to obtain an eternal redemption for
us [*see* Hebrews chapters 8-10]. Praise God forevermore!

I want to encourage you as a Christian to spend most
of your time in the Epistles. I didn't say not to read
elsewhere, for we must. Study the Old Testament, but
spend most of your time in the New Testament. We are
not living under the Old Covenant — we are living under
the New Covenant!

As you read through the Epistles, underline with a red
pencil such expressions as: "in Christ," "by Christ," "in
whom," and "in Him." You will find more than 140; however, some of them don't state benefits or privileges you
have in Christ. For instance, Paul may say, "I greet you
in the name of the Lord Jesus Christ." That has the expres-
sion "in Christ," but it doesn't tell you what is yours
because you are in Christ. Yet there are nearly 130 of these
expressions throughout the Epistles which do tell you
what you have in Christ, or what you are because you are
"in Him," "in Christ," etc.

For instance, Second Corinthians 5:17 is an example
of an "in Christ" Scripture: *"Therefore if any man be in
Christ* [What does he have or what is he because he is in
Christ?], *he is a new creature....*"

Find these Scriptures and then write them down.
Meditate on these Scriptures. Begin to confess them. In
other words, begin to say with your mouth, "This is *who
I am* because I'm in Christ, this is *what I am* in Christ,
and this is *what I have* in Christ." For you see, *faith's*

confessions create reality.

As far as God is concerned, everything you have in Christ and everything you are in Christ is so. God has made all the provisions for you already. However, it is your believing and your confessing who you are in Christ and what you have in Him, that will make them real *to you.*

People have said to me, "Brother Hagin, I read the Bible. I know I am saved. I am born again, filled with the Spirit and speak with other tongues. And yet I cannot grasp the reality of the Word of God. It just doesn't seem real to me."

If the promises and provisions of God's Word never become real to you, they will never do you any good. You see, I can believe there is such a thing as a $100 bill, but it won't do me any good — it won't benefit me personally unless I possess it. Until I make that $100 bill mine, it can't do a thing for me.

The same thing is true of the provisions and promises in God's Word. I can *know* they exist — but I won't be able to possess them with that kind of a general "knowing" or "faith." It is not until I personally appropriate God's promises for myself and put them to work *for me* — that they will benefit my life. Some people have misinterpreted faith. They think that with just a general kind of believing that the promises in God's Word *exist* — they will receive all the benefits of these promises. No, just knowing they exist won't allow you *personally* to enjoy the reality of them. You must meditate on them and confess them, and appropriate them for yourself — to get them to work for you. God wants us to know, to enjoy, and to experience the reality *in our own lives* of all that He has provided for us!

In Him We Have Redemption

HEBREWS 9:12
12 Neither by the blood of goats and calves, but by his own
blood he [Jesus] entered in once into the holy place, having
obtained eternal redemption for us.

We see that God has provided the New Birth — salvation — for us in Jesus' death, burial, and resurrection. Yet
we sometimes talk like this: "So-and-so got saved last
night." But really, from God's viewpoint, God didn't save
that person *then;* He saved him when Jesus was raised
from the dead. That person merely *accepted* the salvation
which Jesus had already provided for him at the cross.
When someone accepts salvation, that's when the provided
redemption actually becomes real *to him.*

Agreeing with God's Word and confessing that it is
so, is the Bible way these truths become real to us. The
Word of God teaches it is with the heart that man believes
— and with the mouth that confession is made in order
to receive the blessings of God (Romans 10:9-10). So when
you believe a thing with your heart and confess it with
your mouth, it becomes real to you. *Faith's confessions
create realities!*

As you read the "in Christ," "in whom," and "in Him"
Scriptures, they may not seem real to you. It may not seem
like you really have what these Scriptures say you have
in Him. But if you will begin to confess (because you do
believe God's Word in your heart), "This is mine. This is
who I am. This is what I have," these Scriptures *will*
become real to you. All that God says you are and all that
God says you have is already real in the spiritual realm.
But you want it to become real in this physical realm so

you can enjoy what's already yours in Christ.

Someone led a blind lady into the healing line one night in one of my meetings. We learned later that she had been totally blind for three years. The minute hands were laid on her, the power of God came upon her, and she fell flat on her back on the floor. She lay still for a few minutes, and when she began to get up we didn't have to ask her whether or not she could see. Her face was lit up like a neon sign. Her eyes were instantly opened and she could see!

Someone said, "God healed that blind woman last night."

Well, no — He really didn't heal her *that* night. He laid her infirmities and diseases on Jesus nearly two thousand years ago and Jesus bore them for her then. She just *accepted* her healing that particular night. But as far as God was concerned, she had already been healed. As far as God was concerned, she really was healed by Jesus' stripes every day she was blind. Her healing was already provided for her in Christ.

MATTHEW 8:17
17 . . . Himself took our infirmities, and bare our sicknesses.

1 PETER 2:24
24 Who his own self bare our sins in his own body on the tree, that we, being dead to sins, should live unto righteousness: by whose stripes ye were healed.

These Scriptures don't say you are *going to be* healed, or there is a *possibility* that you *may be* healed. No, they say, ". . . *ye WERE healed.*"

Getting people to believe these Scriptures in their hearts and confess them with their mouths is the simplest way to get people healed. This will work when nothing else will. God will use special manifestations of the gifts of healings at times, but *God's Word always works!*

Several years ago, a woman was physically carried into one of my services for prayer. She had not walked in four years, and the best doctors in the state said she would never walk again.

Most of the time I minister under the tangible anointing of God's healing power. But when the body gets tired, it is difficult to yield to the anointing and so it will wane, or I will not be so conscious of it.

By the time I came to this woman in the healing line, this was the case. They had brought her from quite a distance, and I knew it would be very difficult for them to bring her back to another meeting.

What was I going to do? Well, thank God, we always have His Word and His Word never fails! So I asked that the woman be brought to the altar. I sat down beside her, laid my opened Bible on her lap, and said, "Sister, would you read that verse outloud?"

She read aloud First Peter 2:24, ending with that last clause, *"by whose stripes ye were healed."*

I then asked her, "Is 'were' past tense, future tense, or present tense?"

I will never forget her reaction. She accepted God's Word the way we all must — with the enthusiasm and simplicity of a little child. Her eyes got big as she looked at me and said, " 'Were' is past tense! If we were healed, *then I was!*"

And that is how God records it. God says that you were healed 2,000 years ago by Jesus' stripes. This is something we have "in Christ." Healing belongs to us because we are in Him!

"Will you do what I tell you?" I asked this crippled woman.

"I will if it is easy."

"It is the easiest thing you ever did. Lift both your hands and begin to praise God. Begin to say, 'I am healed because the Word of God says so.' "

Although she hadn't walked a step, that dear lady lifted her hands and said, "Praise the Lord! Lord, I am so glad I am healed. Lord, I am so glad I can walk again. (She hadn't taken a step yet.) Lord, I am so glad my knees and my limbs are healed. (From all physical evidence they weren't.) I am so glad I can wait on myself. I have been helpless four years, Lord, and I am glad I am not helpless anymore. You know, Lord, how I just had to sit around those four years." (She was still sitting in that wheelchair.) But she was speaking as though it were all a thing of the past.

I said to her, "Rise and walk."

Instantly she leaped to her feet!

She was healed! Someone said, "That Hagin fellow healed a crippled woman last night." Well, I didn't. I didn't have any more to do with healing her than you could have had in healing her. I just brought her the Word of God and she believed it and confessed it. But in the mind of God, in Christ Jesus, she was already healed!

Another woman came to me in a meeting and asked, "Brother Hagin, why don't I get healed? I know healing belongs to me. I know God has promised to heal me. Why doesn't God do what He promised to do?"

I could see her problem, so I tried to help her. I said, "No, God didn't *promise* to heal you."

"Why, Brother Hagin, it says right here in First Peter 2:24, '*by whose stripes ye were healed.*' Doesn't that promise me healing?

"No. That doesn't *promise* you healing at all. That isn't a *promise*. That is a *statement of fact.* First Peter 2:24 *promises* you nothing. It tells you something that has already happened *as a fact.* Jesus took your infirmities. He bore your sicknesses. '*By whose stripes ye were healed.*' That is a fact which tells you that you are already healed."

"No," I said, "God hasn't promised to heal you anymore than He has promised to save the lost. Nowhere in the Bible does God tell us to say to the lost, 'God has promised to save you.' But we are to tell the unsaved, 'God has already done something about your salvation. He laid your sins and your iniquities on Jesus.'"

But she didn't get it. With tears she said, "I know God promised to heal me, and I'm going to keep on praying."

I saw her ten years later and she was still *hoping*. But when the other woman who was crippled *acted* on what was already hers in God's Word, she was able to walk instantly!

Redemptive Rights

EPHESIANS 1:6,7
6   To the praise of the glory of his grace, wherein he hath made us accepted in the beloved.
7   In whom we have redemption through his blood, the forgiveness of sins, according to the riches of his grace.

"*In whom we have redemption. . . .*" Did you ever ask yourself, *From whom or from what are we redeemed?* Some say, "We are redeemed from sin." And that is a part of the story, but it is not the whole story. We are redeemed from the hand of the enemy! We are redeemed from the authority of Satan. But not only that, we are redeemed from the curse of the law!

GALATIANS 3:13
13 Christ hath redeemed us from the curse of the law, being made a curse for us: for it is written, Cursed is every one that hangeth on a tree.

Christ has redeemed us. From what? From the curse of the law. What is the curse of the law? There is only one way to find out. Go back to the law and see what the law says the curse is. Read the 28th chapter of Deuteronomy. Beginning with verse 15, the Bible lists the curse of the law. You will find that the law specifies 11 diseases as being a curse of the law. Then verse 61 encompasses *all* sickness and disease as a curse of the law:

DEUTERONOMY 28:15,61
15 But it shall come to pass, if thou wilt not hearken unto the voice of the Lord thy God, to observe to do all his commandments and his statutes which I command thee this day; that all these curses shall come upon thee, and overtake thee: ...
61 Also every sickness, and every plague, which is not written in the book of this law, them will the Lord bring upon thee [permit], until thou be destroyed.

So the Bible says all sickness and disease is a curse of the law. And it also says that Christ has redeemed us from the curse of the law.

GALATIANS 3:13
13 Christ hath redeemed us from the curse of the law, being

**made a curse for us: for it is written, Cursed is every one
that hangeth on a tree.**

Notice, this Scripture does not say that we are *going
to be* redeemed, but that we are *already* redeemed. We
Christians miss the complete picture of redemption to a
great extent.

The Bible says the same thing in First Peter 2:24: Not
that we are *going to be* healed, but that we *were* healed.
The Bible is looking back to Christ's sacrifice at Calvary
when it says, "*. . . by whose stripes ye were healed.*" God
laid on Jesus not only the iniquities and sins of us all, but
God also laid on Jesus our sicknesses and our diseases.
Jesus bore them for us. Therefore, the Holy Spirit inspired
Peter to write, "*. . . by whose stripes ye WERE healed.*"
As God sees it, we are already healed!

The Ministry of Reconciliation

2 CORINTHIANS 5:17,18
**17 Therefore if any man be in Christ, he is a new creature:
old things are passed away; behold, all things are become
new.**
**18 And all things are of God, who hath reconciled us to
himself by Jesus Christ, and hath given to us the ministry
of reconciliation.**

God has reconciled us to Himself by Christ. *He has
already done it!* And He has given *to us* the ministry of
reconciliation. What is this ministry of reconciliation which
every Christian has? The Bible tells us in Second Corinthians 5:19.

2 CORINTHIANS 5:19
19 To wit, that God was in Christ, reconciling the world

unto himself, not imputing their trespasses unto them; and hath committed unto us the word of reconciliation.

2 CORINTHIANS 5:19 *(Amplified)*
19 It was God (personally present) in Christ, reconciling and restoring the world to favor with Himself, not counting up and holding against [men] their trespasses [but cancelling them]; and committing to us the message of reconciliation — of the restoration to favor.

God was personally present in Jesus Christ, reconciling or restoring the world to favor with Himself. He was not imputing (counting up) or holding against men their trespasses. And He is still not doing that!

When did God cancel man's trespasses? When the sinner comes to God and repents? No! God canceled man's trespasses in Christ at the cross. Reconciliation does not just belong to us Christians who have accepted it! Reconciliation belongs to the world. That's what God wants us to tell them. That's the ministry of reconciliation!

"Well," someone may say, "we'll all be saved then, won't we?"

No. People must lay hold of that reconciliation in order to be saved. Man must be born again because he is by nature a child of the devil. As Jesus said to the Pharisees, *"Ye are of your father the devil..."* (John 8:44). You can see how terrible it is for a man to go to hell when his debt has already been paid!

Some people have read Second Corinthians 5:19, and they've said, "Since God is not holding against man his trespasses — that means everyone will be saved." No! You see, some people take these things too far, take these Scriptures out of their context and then they get off into error.

On one occasion years ago, I picked up a little booklet

that a minister had written. This minister wrote that he'd
had some great "revelation" from God that eventually
everyone would be saved. That didn't come from God —
it came from the devil! He related that he'd had an aunt
who had died years before and he'd wept at her funeral
because he was convinced she went to hell. She was a pros-
titute all of her life and she died drunk. But now, with this
new revelation, he was sure his aunt had gone to heaven.

> **ROMANS 6:23**
> 23 For the wages of sin is death; but the gift of God is eter-
> nal life through Jesus Christ our Lord.
>
> **JOHN 3:16**
> 16 For God so loved the world, that he gave his only begot-
> ten Son, that whosoever believeth in him should not perish,
> but have everlasting life.

No, you see, the Bible says that in order for man to
be saved and go to heaven, he must be born again (John
3:3-8). Man must have a new nature because he is by nature
a child of the devil. Legally speaking, in the mind of God,
God has already accomplished the work through His Son
Jesus at the cross of Calvary for *anyone* to be saved. But
man must accept the finished work of the cross and accept
God's Son, Jesus Christ as his Savior in order to be born
again and have his nature changed.

It is a tragedy for man to be lost when the Good News
is that Christ has already paid the penalty for man's
wrongdoing, and cancelled it out. All anyone has to do is
come and accept the free gift of salvation. The wages of
sin is death. But the gift of God is eternal life! It belongs
to us in Christ Jesus.

The gift of God is eternal life! All a man has to do is

come and accept the gift. That is the Good News! It belongs to us in Jesus.

Scriptural Healing

A man once said to me that First Peter 2:24 meant spiritual healing. But really the Bible doesn't speak of *spiritual* healing.

> **1 PETER 2:24**
> 24 Who his own self bare our sins in his own body on the tree, that we, being dead to sins, should live unto righteousness: by whose stripes ye were HEALED.

> **MARK 5:34**
> 34 And he [Jesus] said unto her, Daughter, thy faith hath made thee WHOLE; go in peace, and be WHOLE of thy plague.

The Greek word translated "healed" in First Peter 2:24 means to heal or to make whole. The Greek word translated "whole" in Mark 5:34 also means to heal. Jesus is talking to the woman with the issue of blood when He says: "... *Daughter, thy faith hath made thee WHOLE; go in peace, and be WHOLE of thy plague.*" According to *Vine's Expository Dictionary of Biblical Words,* both Greek words used in these passages mean the same: To heal and to make whole. These words describe physical healing.

Nowhere does the Bible speak of a man's spirit being "healed." A man's spirit is "born again." A man's body isn't born again, it is healed. Healing is a renewal of the body from a diseased or sick condition. A man's spirit isn't *renewed.* He is born again, born of God. His spirit becomes a new creation in Christ Jesus.

In Him We Are Blessed

EPHESIANS 1:3
3   Blessed be the God and Father of our Lord Jesus Christ,
who hath blessed us with all spiritual blessings in heavenly
places in Christ.

This is one of those "in Christ" Scriptures. Notice God
didn't say He was *going to* bless us with all spiritual blessings, but that He *has already* blessed us with them! That
means that in Christ Jesus, from the time you are born
again until you step into eternity, God has already made
every provision for you for everything you would ever
need. Grasp this mighty truth: God has blessed you with
everything you need in Christ! In the mind of God all
spiritual blessings are already yours.

Find out what belongs to you in Christ. Find out what
your rights and privileges are in Christ. Then begin to confess, "That's mine. That's me. This is what I have in
Christ. This is who I am in Christ. These are the spiritual
blessings I possess in Christ. I have them now!"

Chapter 3
Understanding Righteousness

Fight the good fight of faith....
— 1 Timothy 6:12

The fight of faith is the only one the Christian is called upon to fight. There wouldn't be such a fight to faith if there weren't enemies or hindrances to faith. We need to understand the enemies to faith, and avoid them so that our faith can grow.

ROMANS 10:17
17 So then faith cometh by hearing, and hearing by the word of God.

The greatest enemy or hindrance to faith is a lack of understanding of God's Word, because faith comes by hearing, and hearing by the Word of God. When people pray for faith it's really knowledge of God's Word they need, because we cannot have faith beyond our actual knowledge of God's Word. As soon as the light of God's Word shines in the heart of man, faith comes. That's why the Psalmist said, *"The entrance of thy words giveth light..."* (Ps. 119:130). When you have knowledge of God's Word — you have faith.

Let's investigate one of these hindrances to our faith — the lack of understanding "righteousness," or our right standing with God.

JAMES 5:16-18
16 Confess your faults one to another, and pray one for another, that ye may be healed. The effectual fervent prayer of a RIGHTEOUS man availeth much.

17 Elias [Elijah] was a man subject to like passions as we
are, and he prayed earnestly that it might not rain: and it
rained not on the earth by the space of three years and six
months.
18 And he prayed again, and the heaven gave rain, and the
earth brought forth her fruit.

This passage states that the prayer of a "righteous"
man availeth much. A lack of understanding of what
righteousness is and what privileges righteousness gives
to the believer *holds more Christians in bondage than any
other thing.* In my opinion, righteousness is one of the
most misunderstood subjects in the Bible.

ROMANS 10:10
10 For with the heart man believeth unto righteousness. . . .

ROMANS 5:17
17 For if by one man's offence death reigned by one; much
more they which receive abundance of grace and of the gift
of righteousness shall reign in life by one, Jesus Christ.

Notice that Paul makes two significant statements in
these verses about righteousness:
1. With the *heart* man believes unto righteousness.
2. When we receive Jesus and we are born again, we
   receive "the *gift* of righteousness."
The Bible says in Romans 5:17, that righteousness is
a gift. Too often we have associated righteousness with
good works. The Bible teaches good works and right
conduct, of course, but all of our good works and right
conduct will never make us righteous. If good works could
make us righteous, we wouldn't need Jesus.
Another fallacy about righteousness is that we've
thought we had to grow into some kind of "high" spiritual

state in order to be righteous. We've thought, *My prayers would work if I could just get to be righteous. If I could just develop to some high state of spiritual maturity, then I would be righteous.*

Well, thank God, we can grow in the Lord and we can develop spiritually, but did you know you cannot *grow* in righteousness? There are some things you *can* grow in. For example, you can grow in the fruit of the spirit: love, gentleness, meekness, and longsuffering. But righteousness is a gift. *You will never be any more righteous than you are right now!* You'll not be any more righteous when you get to heaven than you are right now — at this very moment!

Lack of understanding righteousness was one thing that hindered my faith. What can hinder me, can hinder you because we are all human. This very thing, a lack of understanding righteousness — my right standing with God — almost cost me my physical life. It almost caused me to die prematurely. So you can see the importance of fully understanding this subject.

On the bed of sickness more than 50 years ago, after five doctors had given me up to die, I began to read the Bible. I knew if there was any help for me, it had to be in God's Word. My spirit kept telling me I didn't have to die. (You see, your human spirit knows things your head doesn't know; particularly if your spirit has been born of God.) My heart — something on the inside of me — told me there was hope and help for me in God's Word. So I got into the Word with an open mind and I began to see some things about faith and prayer.

I got over to the eleventh chapter of Mark, and read those great statements of faith:

MARK 11:23,24
23 . . . WHOSOEVER shall SAY unto this mountain, Be thou removed, and be thou cast into the sea; and shall not doubt in his heart, but shall believe that those things which he SAITH shall come to pass; he shall have whatsoever he SAITH.
24 Therefore I say unto you, What things soever ye desire, when ye pray, believe that ye receive them, and ye shall have them.

My spirit leaped within me for joy! I was so thrilled. Because it was hard for me to read the entire New Testament through due to my physical condition, I decided to run a reference on Scriptures pertaining to faith and prayer. This brought me to the fifth chapter of James:

JAMES 5:14-16
14 Is any sick among you? let him call for the elders of the church; and let them pray over him, anointing him with oil in the name of the Lord;
15 And the prayer of faith shall save the sick, and the Lord shall raise him up [heal him]; and if he have committed sins, they shall be forgiven him.
16 Confess your faults one to another, and pray one for another, that ye may be healed. The effectual fervent prayer of a righteous man availeth much.

The first thing I noticed, is that James asks a question: *"Is any sick among you?"* (v. 14). By asking a question, James infers that there *might not be* any sick people among them. And, really, if the Church knew and walked in the light of First Peter 2:24, there would not be any sick in the Church! We would be doers of the Word in every area of our lives, including *"By whose stripes ye WERE healed,"* and we would walk in divine health.

Then I read in the next verse about calling for the elders

of the church, and I thought a person *had* to get the elders
to pray in order to be healed. (Actually, you don't *have*
to, but you may.) Tears filled my eyes and I began to cry
because there was no one to call to pray for me.

But the Holy Spirit who is our Teacher called something to my attention. It was so real, it seemed as though
someone spoke up on the inside of me — in my spirit.

The Holy Spirit said, "Did you notice that verse said,
'the prayer of faith shall save the sick'?"

I looked at it again and I said, "Well, yes, that's what
it says."

And that voice within said, "You can pray that prayer
as well as anyone."

I began to see it! I began to believe it!

The Prayer of the Righteous

But when I read further in that same passage about
"the effectual fervent prayer of a RIGHTEOUS man avail-
ing [or working] much," the devil took advantage of my
lack of understanding of God's Word to try to defeat me.
He knew he could defeat me on this point because I didn't
know what righteousness was, nor what privileges it gave
to the believer.

The devil spoke to my mind, and said, "Yes, you could
pray the prayer of faith, *if* you were righteous. But the
Bible says right here, *'The effectual fervent prayer of a
RIGHTEOUS man availeth much.'* If you were righteous,
you could do that — you could pray the prayer of faith
and receive your healing — but you're not righteous."

Notice the devil didn't contradict what the Bible said,
nor did he say, "You *can't* pray the prayer of faith,"

because he knew I recognized my rights in this area. So he used a subtler tactic by reminding me of all my mistakes, faults, and failures, and by telling me I wasn't righteous. He knew I didn't understand righteousness. I thought righteousness was some kind of spiritual state I might eventually attain — *if* I could grow enough spiritually. But I knew I wasn't there yet.

Then the devil bluntly asked me, "Well, *are* you righteous?" I said, "No, no, I'm not." As I looked at myself from the natural standpoint, I wasn't what I considered righteous. I knew I was far from it.

Because I didn't understand my right standing with God and because I accepted what the devil said, I permitted Satan to rob me of the blessings God intended I should have.

I reasoned with myself, *Well, if I can just live long enough to develop spiritually, I could get to be righteous. Then I'd be a "whiz" when it comes to praying.* But I knew I wasn't righteous yet.

This all happened over a period of months. One day I was reading in the Book of James: *"Elias* [Elijah] *was a man subject to like passions as we are . . ."* (James 5:17). I decided to go back and check up on Elijah. He's given to us as an example of a RIGHTEOUS man. Well, if he's an example of a righteous man *praying* and *getting results,* then I can follow him, and I'll get results.

So I began to read up on Elijah, and the more I read, the more he reminded me of myself. Then I remembered that's what James said: *"Elias was a MAN subject to like passions as we are. . . ."* James was comparing Elijah with himself and with the other Christians he was writing to. It wasn't that Elijah had developed to some great degree of spiritual "sainthood," because he was just a man, subject to the same things we are all subject to.

The devil said to me again, "Yes, Elijah was righteous, but *you* are not, so you can't get your prayers answered. You remember this morning how mad you got and knocked that tray off your bed. A *righteous* man doesn't act that way!"

Then I looked back to Elijah who was subject to like passions as we are. Yes, he'd had his *great* moments. By his prayers he'd shut up the heavens from raining for three years and six months (1 Kings 17:1). He'd had that contest with the prophets of Baal and he had prayed down fire. Then, too, he'd prayed the rain down when there was no rain; and when the Spirit of God had come upon him, Elijah had outrun the king's chariot 14 miles across the plains of Jezreel (1 Kings 18:19-46).

But then someone told Elijah, "Jezebel said she's going to have your head cut off by this time tomorrow." (Elijah had previously beheaded 450 prophets of Baal, so now Jezebel was going to have his head.)

So Elijah started running again. When he had run those 14 miles across the plains of Jezreel, the hand of the Lord had been on him. This time, though, when he started running, the hand of the Lord *was not* on him. It was just Elijah running, and he ran until he gave out. Then he crawled under a juniper tree and said, "Lord, just let me die" (1 Kings 19:1-4).

Elijah didn't really want to die. If he had really wanted to die, why didn't he stay where he was? Jezebel would have taken care of that! No, Elijah didn't want to die anymore than some of you did when you said, "I might just as well be dead." You see, Elijah was a man subject to like passions as we are.

As I continued reading, I saw why the Bible said that Elijah was just a man and subject to the same things we are. He talked double-talk sometimes, and he had mistaken ideas. *Elijah is not my idea of a righteous man,* I said to myself. *How in the world could God call Elijah righteous?* I wondered. (But that's where we get into trouble — substituting our ideas for God's Word. If my ideas contradict God's Word, I'll just forget my ideas and get in line with the Word!)

Elijah went on to say, "Lord, you might as well let me die. I'm the only one left anyway. Everyone else is back-slidden but me!" (1 Kings 19:4,10,14).

(You know, you run into that kind of person today too: "No one but me has anything — just me and my little bunch." I'm so glad that's not the truth, aren't you?)

We've all had our mistaken ideas, but in spite of that if we are born again we are righteous in the sight of God, and we can get answers to our prayers.

"Yes," Elijah said, "I'm the only one left; everyone else has bowed their knee to Baal except me."

God had to correct him on that and say, "No, no, I have 7,000 reserved unto myself who have not bowed their knee to Baal" (1 Kings 19:18).

With an attitude like that, how could God call Elijah righteous? How could James, inspired by the Holy Spirit, use this man as *an example* of a righteous man praying? I wondered about that, so I began to check into it.

I found that in the Old Testament, God had set up a system whereby the blood of innocent animals was shed to *cover* the sins of the Old Testament saints. Thus, God did not hold sin against them, but He "counted" them as being righteous.

PSALM 32:1,2
1 Blessed is he whose transgression is forgiven, whose sin is covered.
2 Blessed is the man unto whom the Lord imputeth not iniquity. . . .

Then in the New Testament, I saw that the Bible says we have a *better* Covenant established on *better* promises (Heb. 8:6). In Christian circles we've heard it said, "Our sins are covered." But really our sins aren't *covered.* The New Testament declares we are *cleansed* from sin. Our sins are cleansed — hallelujah — by the blood of the Lord Jesus Christ!

2 CORINTHIANS 5:17
17 Therefore if any man be IN CHRIST, he is a new creature: old things are passed away; behold, all things are become new.

2 CORINTHIANS 5:21
21 For he hath made him [God has made Jesus] to be sin for us, who knew no sin; that we might be made the righteousness of God IN HIM.

Did you notice the phrases "in Christ" and "in Him" in each of these verses? *In Christ* we become *new creatures* (v. 17). *In Him* we become the righteousness of God when we are born again (v. 21). Hallelujah!

When you are born again — when you receive Jesus Christ as your Savior, you become a new man — a new creature in Christ Jesus (2 Cor. 5:17). You know as well as I do that God does not make any "unrighteous" new creatures. That would be an insult to the work of God!

Romans 10:10 says, *"For with the heart man believeth unto righteousness. . . ."* How does a man get righteous? He *believes* unto righteousness — because he believes on Him who is our righteousness — Jesus Christ!

Righteousness — A Gift

Romans 5:17 tells us that we have received an abundance of grace and "the gift of righteousness." Righteousness is a gift! When you were born again, you became a new man in Christ Jesus, and you were made the righteousness of God in Christ (2 Cor. 5:17,21).

When I was teaching on the subject of righteousness years ago in a Full Gospel church in Pennsylvania, the pastor mentioned to me that his Sunday School superintendent was the most spiritual man he'd ever had in his congregation.

The superintendent worked an evening shift, so he attended my day services. He sat on the front seat every morning taking notes. I knew from what the pastor had said that everyone considered this man to be the most dedicated, spiritual Christian in the whole church.

One morning I wanted to illustrate the fact that most people don't know what righteousness is. I suddenly stopped and said to this superintendent, "Are you righteous?"

He said, "I'm trying to be."

"Now, I'm not trying to be vulgar," I said to him, "but are you a man or a woman?"

"I'm a man," he said.

"How did you get that way?" I asked.

He answered, "I was born that way."

I said, "That's the same way you get to be righteous!"
You're *born* righteous, praise God *when you are born
again!* You are made the righteousness of God in Christ
in the New Birth. That's why the Bible says if any man
be in Christ he is a NEW CREATURE (2 Cor. 5:17). That's
also why the Bible compares being a new creature to the
innocence of a new-born babe. *"AS NEWBORN BABES,
desire the sincere milk of the word, that ye may grow
thereby"* (1 Peter 2:2). The Bible teaches that there is a
similarity between spiritual growth and physical growth.
Christians are born babies, and they grow up. And those
who are newly born again into the Kingdom of God are
just as righteous in the sight of God as older saints who
have been born again and living for God 50 or 60 years,
and are full of good works and right conduct. Those newborn babes can get their prayers answered just as quickly
as older saints — because righteousness means *right standing with God!* We must realize, too, that we have right
standing with God not because of what *we* did, but because
of what *Jesus* did! Right standing with God is a gift! We
have received the gift of righteousness in Christ Jesus.
Receive the gift!

You'll not have any better standing with God when you
get to heaven than you do right now. Hallelujah! That's
difficult for some people to accept. But if they believe what
the Bible says, they'll have to accept it. Sometimes we get
"religious" teachings confused with actual Biblical, New
Testament teachings.

Let's read again Second Corinthians 5:21: *"For he hath
made him* [Jesus] *to be sin for us, who knew no sin. . . ."*
I believe this part of the verse is true, don't you?

I've read this first part of that verse in services and

then asked the people: "How many of you believe this part of the verse is true?" Everyone lifted their hands.

Then I would read the last part of the same verse: "*. . . that we might be made the righteousness of God in him* [Christ]." I would say to them, "We are the righteousness of God in Christ. How many of you believe that's true?"

Most of the time, only half of the people would lift their hands! Yet if the first half of that verse is true, the last half must be true too. You see, God has already made a provision which belongs to us — righteousness! We need to realize that righteousness is ours and begin to walk in the light of it!

ROMANS 3:21-26
21 But now the righteousness of God [Remember, we are made the righteousness of God in Christ.] without the law is manifested, being witnessed by the law and the prophets;
22 Even the righteousness of God which is by faith of Jesus Christ unto all and upon ALL THEM THAT BELIEVE [That sets something dancing on the inside of me!]: for there is no difference:
23 For all have sinned, and come short of the glory of God;
24 Being justified freely by his grace through the redemption that is in Christ Jesus:
25 Whom God hath set forth to be a propitiation [the atoning sacrifice] through faith in his blood, to declare his righteousness for the remission of sins that are past, through the forbearance of God;
26 To declare, I say, at this time his righteousness: that he might be just, and the justifier of him which believeth in Jesus.

The Greek word "righteous" can also be translated "just." *The Amplified Bible* says that God ". . . justifies

and accepts as righteous him who has [true] faith in Jesus"
(v. 26).

> **ROMANS 5:17-21**
> 17 For if by one man's offence [That's Adam's sin in the
> beginning.] **death reigned by one** [Because of Adam's sin,
> Satan reigned through spiritual death — not physical
> death.] ; **much more they which receive abundance of grace
> and of the gift of righteousness shall reign in life by one,
> Jesus Christ.**
> 18 Therefore as by the offence of one judgment came upon
> all men to condemnation; even so by the righteousness of
> one [That's Jesus and His righteousness.] the free gift came
> upon all men unto justification of life. [Or unto
> "righteousness of life" because the Greek word is the same.]
> 19 For as by one man's disobedience many were made sin-
> ners, so by the obedience of one shall many be made
> righteous.
> 20 Moreover the law entered, that the offence might
> abound. But where sin abounded, grace did much more
> abound:
> 21 That as sin hath reigned unto death, even so might
> grace reign through righteousness unto eternal life by Jesus
> Christ our Lord.

Going back to the seventeenth verse, we see that we
have received abundance of grace and we have received
the gift of righteousness. Righteousness, then, is a gift.
Righteousness is right standing with God!

Benefits of Righteousness: Reigning in Life

What privileges does righteousness give to the
believer? The seventeenth verse tells us one of the benefits
of righteousness: "... *they which receive abundance of
grace and of the gift of righteousness SHALL REIGN IN*

LIFE. . . . " We shall reign in life — that means in this life right here on earth!

One of our problems is that we've wanted to relegate everything to the future and not enjoy our privileges in Christ right now. This attitude is reflected in the songs we sing, such as "When We All Get to Heaven." Well, thank God, we're going to heaven and it will be wonderful, but we don't have to wait until we get there to enjoy the rights and privileges we have in Christ! Praise God, we can enjoy them *now.* And, thank God, we will reign with Christ in eternity, but we don't have to wait until then to start reigning.

The Amplified Bible says that we shall ". . . reign as kings in life through the One, Jesus Christ, the Messiah, the Anointed One" (v. 17). *Where* are we going to reign as kings? *In life* — that means in this life! How? By Jesus Christ!

Paul used this illustration because in the day he wrote, there were kings. There aren't many kings left today, and those kings who do remain don't have much authority or power. But in those days, many nations had kings, and the king's word was the final authority in his domain.

We need to grasp this truth: The Word of God says *we* shall reign as kings in life by Christ Jesus! That means we have authority *in this life!* How can we reign? Because we have been made the righteousness of God in Christ! Jesus who is righteous became our righteousness. Because of Jesus we have right standing with God. Our standing with God is secure:

We can stand in the presence of God as though we had never done wrong.

We can stand in the presence of God as though we had

never sinned.

We can stand in the presence of God without a sense of condemnation or inferiority.

No wonder it says in Hebrews: *"Let us therefore come boldly unto the throne of grace, that we may obtain mercy, and find grace to help in time of need"* (Heb. 4:16). We can come boldly to the throne of God, all because of what Jesus has done for us!

Authority Over Satan

In this life, we run up against Satan on every side. In Second Corinthians 4:4 the Bible says Satan is the god of this world. But we can stand in the presence of Satan — right before him — without fear. He can't condemn us. When you know the truth, you can stand in the presence of Satan with authority. That authority gives you dominion over Satan, over demons, and over disease because you know that you stand *in Jesus.* Hallelujah! Satan knows that too.

When I began to see this, I realized that Satan had been defeating me because of my lack of knowledge and my lack of understanding of righteousness. I began to say, "I am the righteousness of God in Christ. I am that righteous man James was talking about when he said, *'The effectual fervent prayer of a RIGHTEOUS man availeth much' "* (James 5:16).

Earlier I'd said, "If I ever get to be righteous, I'll be a 'whiz' at praying." So now I wrote beside this verse in my Bible, "I am a whiz at prayer!"

And you are, too, if you just knew it and would take advantage of it! Sometimes people think spiritual things are just going to work automatically. But something can be yours spiritually, just like it can be in the natural, but if you don't know it, it won't profit you anything. It is *acting upon knowledge* that brings results. It is acting upon *what already belongs* to you that brings results!

Wouldn't it be foolish for someone to come into a unlit room, grope around in the dark, finally find a chair and sit down, and then grumble, "Why isn't there any light in this room?" Sometimes people are that foolish when it comes to spiritual things too. They go without the blessings of God because they fail to act upon what already belongs to them, and then they complain, "If God has promised to bless me, why hasn't He?" We must remember, there's a part we play in receiving the blessings of God!

The lights go on only when someone acts on what they know! When someone finds out where the light switch is *and turns it on* — that's when there's light. It's the same way in the spiritual realm. *When you find out what God's Word says and act on it, that's when you get results!*

Act on What You Know

Take your place in Jesus Christ. When you know this truth, you won't have to be running around to get someone else to do your praying for you. You'll know that God hears you just as quickly as He hears anyone else. He hears your prayer because your standing with Him is just as good as any other Christian's.

An evangelist, pastor, or minister doesn't have any better standing with God than you do. A minister just has a *duty* or a *responsibility* which you don't have. But that responsibility doesn't make him any more *righteous* or give him any better standing with God. God won't hear him pray or answer his prayer any quicker than He'll hear and answer your prayer.

You see, God doesn't love one member of the Body of Christ more than another. We've got all kinds of wrong ideas about this, such as "If I could just get a *real* man of God to pray for me, God would answer." No, some Christians may have learned how to take advantage of what belongs to them better than you have, but they are not any more *righteous* than you are. God won't hear them pray any more quickly than He'll hear you pray.

I'm thoroughly convinced that there are going to arise in these last days, bands of believers who will learn how to take their place in Christ knowing who and what they are in Him. Talk about prayer warriors! Talk about consecrated, dedicated lives of prayer! Talk about getting results — they are going to get them! They won't have to be dependent on someone else to pray in order to get answers for them.

God will hear *you!* In our churches we've been trained to leave it up to the pastor to do all the praying. But when you gain understanding of what righteousness is and what it means to you, you will be able to step out from that narrow place of theology where you have lived and step into the boundless fullness of God!

Some people say, "I can see from the Word of God that we've received remission of sins that are past and we've received the gift of righteousness. I can see that we've been made righteous new creatures, but what about those sins and wrongdoings I've committed since I've become a Christian?"

Satan used this very thing to defeat me after I'd
learned these facts about righteousness from the Bible.
He said, "Yes, that's right, you were made a new creature
in Christ and God doesn't make any unrighteous new
creatures. But since you've been saved, you've sinned.
Remember when you got angry and lost your temper?"
(He knew he could no longer dispute my righteousness,
because the Word is true and I'd discovered the truth.)

So now Satan tried to trip me up by using the fact that
since becoming a Christian, I'd sinned. I felt so guilty that
I'd missed it. Have you ever missed it since you became
a Christian? Since you've been saved, have you ever failed,
sinned, or missed it?

But I began to look at the Word again, and I found
this verse in First John:

1 JOHN 1:9
9   If we confess our sins, he is faithful and just to forgive
us our sins, and to cleanse us from all unrighteousness.

John wasn't writing to *sinners* here. He was writing
to Christians because he called them "my little children."

1 JOHN 2:1,2
1   My little children, these things write I unto you, that
ye sin not. And if any man sin, we have an advocate with
the Father, Jesus Christ the righteous:
2   And he is the propitiation [the atoning sacrifice] for our
sins: and not for ours only, but also for the sins of the whole
world.

When a man sins, he is under condemnation and he
loses his *sense* of righteousness. But when he confesses,
"I've sinned and I've failed You, God. Please forgive me

Lord, in Jesus' Name," God does two things. According to First John 1:9, God *forgives* us of our sins, and God *cleanses* us from our sins. If God just forgave us our sin it wouldn't help us much, because we would still be under the condemnation of sin. But, no, God actually *cleanses us from all sin.* (For more on the subject of remission and forgiveness, refer to my minibook *Three Big Words.)*

What does God cleanse us from? ALL unrighteousness. *All* unrighteousness! Part of our unrighteousness? No, *all* of it.

After I saw this in the Word, I came back to the devil with that news and put him on the run. He's been running ever since. Up until then the devil had me on the run. If I saw the devil anywhere, I'd cross the street in the middle of the block just to keep from meeting him. I'd go down the back alley just so I wouldn't run into him. (I'm speaking figuratively, you understand.) If he popped his head up anywhere, brother, I was ready to turn and run. But after I found out who I am in Christ Jesus, praise God, I almost invited him to come by my house! If I see him, I meet him head on — and now he's the one who turns and runs, because he found out that I know what the Word says!

Chapter 4
Understanding Our Legal Right
to the Name of Jesus

Fight the good fight of faith....
— 1 Timothy 6:12

If there is a fight to faith, it follows that there are enemies to faith. And as we have pointed out previously, the greatest enemy to faith is a lack of knowledge of God's Word.

The Bible tells us, *". . . faith cometh by hearing, and hearing by the word of God"* (Rom. 10:17). You can readily see that a lack of knowledge of God's Word would be the greatest hindrance to faith there is.

In my own case, as soon as I found out what God's Word said along certain lines, my faith was no longer hindered. The only thing in my life that ever hindered my faith was a lack of knowledge of God's Word. As soon as I got knowledge of God's Word, my lack of understanding straightened out and my faith worked! It will be the same with you.

We have been studying six big hindrances to faith. The fourth hindrance to faith which we will look at in this chapter is the lack of understanding of our legal right to the use of the Name of Jesus. Not understanding our legal right to use that Name holds us in bondage and gives us a sense of weakness. But by knowing what the Name will do, we can defeat Satan and enjoy victory every single time! How wonderful that the Name of Jesus belongs to the Church! It belongs to every member — even the least and weakest member — of the Body of Christ.

Let's find out what the Word of God has to say about

Jesus and His Name. The Word will then build faith into our spirits, our hearts, and our inner man.

We will begin with the first chapter of Hebrews. This passage is speaking of Jesus, because it says, *"Who being the brightness of his* [God's] *glory, and the express image of his* [God's] *person . . . "* (Heb. 1:3). Jesus is the brightness of God's glory and the express image of God's person. He is the very outshining of God the Father.

> **HEBREWS 1:3-7**
> 3 Who being the brightness of his glory, and the express image of his person, and upholding all things by the word of his power, when he had by himself purged our sins, sat down on the right hand of the Majesty on high;
> 4 Being made so much better than the angels, as he hath by inheritance obtained A MORE EXCELLENT NAME than they.
> 5 For unto which of the angels said he at any time, Thou art my son, this day have I begotten thee? And again, I will be to him a Father, and he shall be to me a Son?
> 6 And again, when he bringeth in the firstbegotten into the world, he saith, And let all the angels of God worship him.
> 7 And of the angels he saith, Who maketh his angels spirits, and his ministers a flame of fire.

Now let's read Ephesians 1:19-23. Take time to meditate on these verses. Think on them. Feed on them until they become a part of your inner consciousness. If you will take time to meditate on the Word, it will do something for you. But if you just casually read these Scriptures and let them get away from you, they won't mean anything *to you* or be able to accomplish anything *for you.*

EPHESIANS 1:19-23

19 And what is the exceeding greatness of his power to usward who believe, according to the working of his mighty power,

20 Which he wrought in Christ, when he raised him from the dead, and set him at his own right hand in the heavenly places,

21 FAR ABOVE all principality, and power, and might, and dominion, and EVERY NAME that is named, not only in this world, but also in that which is to come:

22 And hath put all things under his feet, and gave him to be the head over all things to the church,

23 Which is his body, the fulness of him that filleth all in all.

PHILIPPIANS 2:8-11

8   And being found in fashion as a man, he humbled himself, and became obedient unto death, even the death of the cross.

9   Wherefore God also hath highly exalted him, and given him a NAME which is above every name:

10 That AT THE NAME of Jesus every knee should bow, of things in heaven, and things in earth, and things under the earth;

11 And that every tongue should confess that Jesus Christ is Lord, to the glory of God the Father.

The *Rotherham* translation of Philippians 2:10 reads, "In order that in the name of Jesus every knee might bow of beings in heaven, and on earth, and underground." This means angels, men, and demons must bow to the Name of Jesus. Notice in Philippians 2:8,9 that it was after Jesus' resurrection when His Name was conferred upon Him. After Jesus' resurrection was when God highly exalted Jesus.

Jesus' Name Belongs to the Church

Now let's consider this question: Why was this Name conferred upon Jesus? In these Scriptures, it says that God raised Jesus up and gave Him a Name which is above all dominion, all authority, and all power. It says that God has highly exalted Jesus and seated Jesus at His own right hand far above all dominion and all authority and all power. Why was this Name invested with such authority and dominion? Was it done for Jesus' benefit? No!

During the 2,000 years since the resurrection of the Lord Jesus Christ and His ascension and seating on High at the right hand of the Father, Jesus has not used that Name once! The Scriptures do not give us any indication that Jesus Himself has ever used the Name. He has no need to use the Name! Jesus rules creation by His Word, because He is equal with God.

This is what I want you to see: At its every mention in the Scriptures — we see that the Name of Jesus has been given *to the Church* to use! Every mention of the use of the Name is in reference to the Body of Christ!

For purposes of study, let's connect these verses that pertain to the Name:

HEBREWS 1:4
4 Being made so much better than the angels, as he hath by inheritance obtained a more excellent NAME than they.

EPHESIANS 1:19-21
19 ... what is the exceeding greatness of his power....
20 Which he wrought in Christ, when he raised him from the dead, and set him at his own right hand in the heavenly places,

21 FAR ABOVE all principality, and power, and might, and dominion, and EVERY NAME THAT IS NAMED, not only in this world, but also in that which is to come.

PHILIPPIANS 2:9,10
9   Wherefore God also hath highly exalted him, and given him a NAME which is above every name:
10 That at the NAME of Jesus every knee should bow, of things in heaven, and things in earth, and things under the earth.

Now we need to see that the Name belongs to the Church:

EPHESIANS 1:21-23
21 [Jesus and His Name are] Far above all principality, and power, and might, and dominion, and every name that is named, not only in this world, but also in that which is to come:
22 And hath put all things under his feet, and gave him to be the head over all things to the CHURCH,
23 Which is his body, the fulness of him that filleth all in all.

The Name of Jesus belongs to the Church, the Body of Christ!

1 CORINTHIANS 12:27,28
27 Now ye are the BODY OF CHRIST, and members in particular.
28 And God hath set some in the CHURCH. . . .

In this 27th verse, the Bible says, *"ye are the body of Christ,"* and in the very next verse, the Body of Christ is called the Church.

Every mention in the Scriptures of the use of the Name of Jesus refers to its being used by His Body, the Church.

The Name was given to Jesus so that His Body — the Church — could use it. So the Name which is above every name belongs to me and it belongs to you! We need to realize that *according to God's Word* that Name *legally* belongs to us.

What are we doing about the Name?

Proper Use of Jesus' Name

Remember that old song we used to sing, "Take the name of Jesus with you, child of sorrow and of woe"? That's not us! That does not describe the Body of Christ, the Church of the Lord Jesus Christ! We are not children of sorrow and of woe. We belong to the King of kings. There was also another song that used the phrase: "Here I wander like a beggar through the heat and through the cold. . . ." Well, in the first place, we are not beggars. The Bible says we are heirs of God — sons of God — and joint-heirs with Jesus Christ.

In the second place, we are not wandering. We know exactly who we are and where we are going, praise God! One reason our faith has been hindered in the Body of Christ is because some of our songs have been embalmed with such unbelief.

We in the Body of Christ have sung songs that really are unscriptural. And we've sung them so long we think they are the truth! Some are part scripture, part sentiment, and part unbelief. But they are not the truth — God's Word is truth!

We need to stop and think sometimes about the effect the songs that we sing have on us spiritually. That's the trouble with us humans sometimes: We just follow blindly on without doing any thinking.

We have done the same thing with the Name of Jesus: We have not realized the full importance of the Name. I think some have thought that we are just to take Jesus' Name along with us like a good luck charm; that the Name would work like a rabbit's foot or a horseshoe hanging over the door. But it doesn't work that way. Yes, the Name is given to us for our use. But we could take it along with us and never use it. And if we don't use it, the Name will never mean anything *to us* or be able to do anything *for us*.

The Name of Jesus has been given to the Body of Christ for our benefit. God has made an investment with that Name for the Church. God has made a deposit — the Name of Jesus — from which the Church has the right to draw for her every need.

PHILIPPIANS 4:19
19 But my God shall supply all your need according to his riches in glory by Christ Jesus.

You see, the Name — this wonderful Name — the Name of Jesus, has within it the fullness of the Godhead. The Name has within it all the wealth of eternity. The Name has within it all authority and power over all the powers of darkness. And that Name belongs to us!

Praying in Jesus' Name

Now let's study how Jesus said we could use His Name. Jesus is saying in John 16:23,24 that the Church, the Body of Christ, has the right to come before the Father with that Name — *to use His Name in prayer.*

JOHN 16:23,24
23 And in that day ye shall ask me nothing. Verily, verily,
I say unto you, Whatsoever ye shall ask the Father IN MY
NAME he will give it you.
24 Hitherto have ye asked nothing in my name: ask, and
ye shall receive, that your joy may be full.

Jesus said this to His disciples just before He went to
the cross. He began with the phrase, *"In that day...."*
He was not speaking to them about the very hour in which
they were living. No, Jesus was looking forward to another
day. Jesus was looking forward to the *"In that day"* —
after He would have gone to the cross ... died ... been
buried ... been raised from the dead ... ascended on High
... and sat down at the right hand of the Father. *"In that
day"* is the day we are living in now; it is the day of the
New Covenant — the day of the New Testament!

Jesus said, *"In that day* [of the New Covenant] *ye shall
ask me nothing...* [But] *Whatsoever ye ... ask the Father
in my name, he will give it you."* This promise is one of
the most staggering statements that ever fell from the lips
of Jesus. This Scripture is the charter promise given to
the Church regarding our rights in prayer.

Jesus continued with the word "hitherto." *"Hitherto
have ye asked nothing in my name..."* (John 16:24).
Hitherto means "up to now"; "until now" or "until this
time." You see, when Jesus was here on the earth no one
prayed in His Name to God the Father. It was only after
Jesus' death, burial, and resurrection, when He was
exalted on High and seated at the right hand of God the
Father, that the power and authority in that Name was
conferred upon Him. And so Jesus said, *"Hitherto* [or up
until now] *have ye asked nothing in my name: ask*

[Hallelujah! He told us to ask!], *and ye shall receive, that your joy may be full."*

Our Right to Jesus' Name

Jesus is saying that believers, the Body of Christ, the Church — you and I — have the right to come in that Name to the Father. Jesus is telling us that we are to use His Name in prayer.

Also notice in John 16:23,24 that Jesus does not mention *faith* or *believing.* He does not say, "If you *believe,* the Father will grant your request," or "If you have *faith,* the Father will give you what you need." No, Jesus says, *"Whatsoever ye shall ask the Father IN MY NAME, he will give it you"!*

You see, Jesus has given us His Name. It's legally ours to use, and what is ours doesn't take faith to use. To say it another way, I drive an automobile. My car belongs to me; I possess the keys to it. It does not take faith for me to put the key in the ignition and drive away. I'm just using what already belongs to me. I don't need to turn in a prayer request every time I want to drive my car, asking the congregation to pray for me so I'll have the faith to put the key in the ignition to drive home.

No, the car belongs to me. I simply use what already belongs to me! The Name of Jesus is the same way: It's already yours. The Name has been given to the Church to use. Use what already belongs to you!

When you were born into the family of God, the right and the privilege to use the Name of Jesus became yours. It did take *faith* to get into the family of God because, *"by grace are ye saved through faith. . ."* (Eph. 2:8). But once you are born again into the family of God, everything that Jesus has bought and paid for — everything He has purchased — automatically belongs to you. It is all yours because you are in the family of God!

Consider those carnal Christians at Corinth. Paul calls them "carnal" or as one translation reads, "body-ruled" Christians. Most people wouldn't think these Corinthians could get anything from God because they were carnal. Yet Paul said to them, *". . . all things are yours . . . And ye are Christ's; and Christ is God's"* (1 Cor. 3:21,23).

Use What Is Yours

"All things are yours." Notice that it does *not* say all things are *going to become* yours. They already belong to you! But it is up to you to use what belongs to you.

We can see an instance of this in the story of the prodigal son (Luke 15:11-32). Remember the elder brother who came in from the field? He heard the sound of music and dancing in celebration because they were having a banquet. He asked some of the servants what was going on and they told him, "Your brother, the prodigal, has come home and your father has made a feast for him. He has put a robe on him, shoes on his feet, a ring on his finger, and has killed the fatted calf and made a feast for him." The elder son got mad about it and wouldn't go in to the feast, so his father came out and entreated him.

If that prodigal son is a type of the sinner or backslider, and the father is a type of God, then the elder brother is a type of a Christian who has not strayed away. And when the father came out and entreated him to come in and join the feast, the elder brother said, "No, I am not coming in. I have served you faithfully all these years. I never went away from you. I didn't go off and spend your money in riotous living. But you have never made a feast for me. You have never killed any fatted calf for me. You have never let me invite my friends in to have a feast." And the father replied, "Why, Son, ALL I HAVE IS YOURS" (Luke 15:31).

It's strange, but that Scripture often falls on deaf ears. *What most people are praying for is already theirs* if they just knew how to take hold of it through the Name of Jesus! Sometimes they are like the elder brother. Backsliders or sinners can come in, get right with God, and be blessed instantly appropriating what belongs to them in Christ, and these people almost get mad about it.

I remember one instance in particular along this line. Two Methodist women came to a meeting we were holding in a Full Gospel church. Doctors had given one of these women only six months to live. This woman was carried into the meeting and she was carried out of the meeting. She was not healed instantly. But within two days of hearing the Word preached, every symptom left her body, and she came walking into that meeting by herself! (I saw her ten years later and she was still perfectly healed.) Then the other woman, her mother-in-law who'd had two strokes and was in a wheelchair, was healed instantly and walked out of that wheelchair.

After the meeting, one of the women in that Full Gospel church came to me with tears and said, "Brother Hagin, can you tell me something? How come God healed those two Methodist women and He won't heal me? They haven't even got the Holy Spirit. They don't even speak in tongues. I talk in tongues. Why won't God heal me?"

Trying to get her to see that healing already belonged to her, I said, "Sister, God has done all He is ever going to do about healing you."

"You mean He's not going to heal me?"

"I didn't say that. I said He has done all He is ever going to do about healing you. You see, He has already laid your sickness on Jesus and Jesus bore your sicknesses on the cross; Jesus carried your diseases, and by His stripes you *were* healed. As far as God is concerned, you are already healed."

"Well, I just believe," she said, "that sometime, somewhere, in God's own good way, when He gets ready, He is going to heal me." She went down the road mumbling to herself. I don't mean to be unkind about it, but that's not the right road. Five years and then ten years later I saw her and she was still sick.

Now the two Methodist women who were healed knew nothing about what legally belonged to them in Christ; but like the prodigal, when they saw that healing was theirs, they came in and had a feast. The "elder sister," though, came in from the fields and got mad about it. And the Father was trying to say to her, "Why, daughter, *all I have is thine.*"

All you have to do is ask yourself this question: *Does God have whatever I need?* Because He does have it, then it is already yours!

God Has Already Done It All

One preacher said, "I didn't think I was ever going to

talk God into saving me. It took me three days and nights." How ridiculous! God's Word says in Revelation 13:8, that Christ was the Lamb slain before the foundation of the world. Here this fellow was trying to talk God into the notion of saving him, and God had his salvation all planned and figured out before the foundation of the world! Salvation — man's *redemption* — is why the Lamb came. The Bible says, *"For the Son of man is come to seek and to save that which was lost"* (Luke 19:10).

Another man said, "I tell you, I thought God was never going to baptize me in the Holy Ghost. I never thought I would get God in the notion of giving me the Holy Spirit."

Oh, my, my, my. It might be funny if it weren't so pathetic. You don't have to talk God into the notion of anything. God is already in the notion! God has already made provision for everything you need. Furthermore, God has given you the Name of Jesus to use for your every need. That Name guarantees an answer!

Demanding in Jesus' Name

An example of demanding in Jesus' Name is seen at the Gate called Beautiful in Acts 3:1-9.

ACTS 3:1-9
1   Now Peter and John went up together into the temple at the hour of prayer, being the ninth hour.
2   And a certain man lame from his mother's womb was carried, whom they laid daily at the gate of the temple which is called Beautiful, to ask alms of them that entered into the temple;
3   Who seeing Peter and John about to go into the temple asked an alms.

4   And Peter, fastening his eyes upon him with John, said, Look on us.
5   And he gave heed unto them, expecting to receive something of them.
6   Then Peter said, Silver and gold have I none; but such as I have give I thee: IN THE NAME of Jesus Christ of Nazareth rise up and walk.
7   And he took him by the right hand, and lifted him up: and immediately his feet and ankle bones received strength.
8   And he leaping up stood, and walked, and entered with them into the temple, walking, and leaping, and praising God.
9   And all the people saw him walking and praising God.

Did you notice that the disciples did not *pray* to the Father in the Name of Jesus to get this man healed? Did you ever notice in reading the New Testament that the disciples did not *pray* for people to be healed? People can be healed through prayer, but the disciples didn't pray for people to be healed. The disciples just exercised their authority in that Name. At the Gate Beautiful, Peter said, "IN THE NAME of Jesus, arise and walk." Peter asked or *demanded* that the man get up and walk in the Name of Jesus, and the man did!

Do you see this important truth: We have *the authority* to use Jesus' Name! God's power is in that Name! And when we use that Name, it is just as though Jesus were here Himself. All the power and all the authority that is invested in Jesus *is in that Name!* Hallelujah!

You see, you are not demanding anything of the Father. It wasn't God the Father who made that man crippled or who bound him. The devil did that. Jesus' Name belongs to you and if Satan attacks you, you have the right to demand in the Name of Jesus that he leave you alone. If pain comes to your body, demand in the Name of Jesus that it leave you. That Name *belongs* to you!

Believers' Use of the Name

In Mark 16:15 Jesus said, *"Go ye into all the world, and preach the gospel. . . ."* Then He also said:

MARK 16:17,18
17 And these signs shall follow them that believe [the believing ones]; **IN MY NAME** shall they cast out devils; they shall speak with new tongues;
18 They shall take up serpents; and if they drink any deadly thing, it shall not hurt them; they shall lay hands on the sick, and they shall recover.

Jesus delegated the power and authority in that Name to *the believing ones*. That's us — the Body of Christ! Some have relegated the use of the Name to those specially used of God in the gifts of the Spirit, for instance. But this isn't just talking about evangelists, or pastors, or someone who is used in the gifts of the Spirit. This verse is talking about the entire Body of Christ — the believing ones — they all have the power and authority to use the Name. *"These signs shall follow them that BELIEVE; In my name . . ."* (v. 17). Or as the literal Greek says, "These signs shall follow the believing ones."

There is authority invested in the Name of Jesus. There is authority invested in the Church of the Lord Jesus Christ. Some of us have touched that now and then. None of us have been able to abide in it like God wants us to.

But I am thoroughly convinced and I firmly believe that in these last days, just before Jesus comes, there will arise a body of believers who will learn how to take advantage of what belongs to them — and will know how to use Jesus' Name — the Name that is above every name!

Chapter 5
Understanding
How To Act on God's Word

Fight the good fight of faith....
— 1 Timothy 6:12

The only fight the Christian is called upon to fight is the faith fight. If we are in any other kind of fight, we are in the wrong fight. We need to get out of the wrong fight and get into the right one.

Some Christians say, "I'm going to fight the devil." There's no need to do that. Jesus already defeated him. You wouldn't be any match for him anyway. Because Jesus has already defeated Satan for you, there is no use for *you* to fight the devil.

Some say, "I'm going to fight sin." There is no need to do that either, because Jesus has the *cure* for sin. The cure for sin *is* Jesus, praise God. Jesus put away sin by the sacrifice of Himself according to Hebrews 9:26. So there really isn't *a sin* problem. There is just *a sinner* problem, and when you get the sinner to Jesus, Jesus cures that.

There are enemies in this fight of faith which we are instructed to fight. If there were no enemies or hindrances to faith, there would be no fight to it.

Hindrances to Faith

We have seen that hindrances to faith exist because of a lack of knowledge of God's Word. Romans 10:17 states, "... *faith cometh by hearing, and hearing by the word of God.*"

77

People often pray for faith, saying "What I need is faith." But actually what they need is knowledge of God's Word.

When the knowledge of God's Word comes, faith automatically comes. You could pray for faith forever, but if you didn't get any knowledge of God's Word, you would never get faith. This is because ". . . *faith cometh by hearing, and hearing by the word of God.*" If you could get faith in any other way, this Scripture would be a lie. And if there is even one Scripture in the Bible that is a lie, then the whole Bible is a lie. But I am glad that the Bible is all true.

You can see that the greatest hindrance to faith is a lack of understanding of the Word of God. The hindrance we will discuss in this chapter is one which holds many in bondage. Our faith is held in bondage because we lack understanding of *how to act on God's Word.*

Trying To Believe

You see, some Christians *try* to believe, and it is such a struggle for them. They say they are "*trying* to have faith," or "*trying* to believe." All that is necessary, however, is to act on what God says in His Word. If we know the Word of God is true *and* act on it, then it becomes a reality in our lives.

Real faith is a product of the knowledge of the Word of God. It takes no effort whatsoever on the part of the intellect or the will of man to obtain faith. As soon as the light of God's Word comes, faith is there. Faith is the concomitant of knowledge. That is, faith accompanies knowledge. Knowledge of God's Word comes first — then faith automatically accompanies it.

As the Psalmist of old said, *"The entrance of THY WORDS giveth light . . ."* (Ps. 119:130). As soon as the *light* of God's Word comes, faith is there. So feed on God's Word. Meditate on God's Word. Feeding and meditating on God's Word will bring the light, and it will bring faith because, *". . . faith cometh by hearing, and hearing by the word of God."*

I use the phrase "acting on God's Word" rather than the terms "have faith" or "believe" because that is what faith actually is: Faith is simply *acting* on God's Word.

Someone asked Raymond T. Richey, a man mightily used of God in years gone by in the healing ministry, "What is faith?" His reply was, "Faith is just acting on God's Word." And that's all it is. Smith Wigglesworth would say, "Faith is an act." Faith *is* an act. That's what faith is — faith is acting on God's Word. Faith is acting like God's Word is true.

Mental Assent

Many times we unknowingly make a substitution for faith. We substitute "mental assent" or "mental agreement" for faith. For instance, we mentally agree that God's Word is true, and we think we are believing and that we are in faith — but we are not. You can mentally assent or mentally agree all day long that the Bible is true, but the Word does not become real to you until you act on it. It is only when you act on God's Word for yourself that it becomes a reality *to you.* And it is only when you act on God's Word that you are exercising *faith.*

For example, you can hold to the resurrection truth as

a great doctrine (and in some circles that's about all it is — a doctrine or a dogma), but it will not mean a thing to you until you can believe in your heart and say with your mouth, "Jesus died for me. Jesus was raised from the dead for *me!* Jesus arose victorious over death, hell, and the grave — and He did it all for *me!* Praise God forevermore! Jesus arose victorious over Satan! Jesus arose a victor! Jesus conquered Satan for *me,* and therefore Satan has no dominion over me! I'm free! Praise God, I'm free! Satan has no dominion over me! I'm free!"

It is when you believe it in your heart and confess it with your mouth — that is when the resurrection truth in the Word of God becomes something more than just a doctrine, more than just a dogma, more than just a creed, more than just a theory — it becomes a reality to you. The Word of God won't mean a thing to you until you can say these Biblical truths with your mouth, and believe them in your heart. Remember, the people who get answers from God, are those who *act* on His Word.

Act Like the Bible Is True

I pastored almost 12 years and I found that in a church you have the same type of problems that you have in a family, because the church is made up of families. In families, financial and discipline problems arise. In the church you also have financial problems and discipline problems. In the church you have all the problems you have wherever people are involved.

During those 12 years of pastoral work, we faced the same problems you do in your homes and families. The crises of life come to us all. And if, when the crises of life come, you do not know how to act on God's Word, you are at a disadvantage.

In one church I pastored, as we were discussing church problems, the board of deacons said to me, "What are we going to do now?" I just smiled and said, "We're just going to act like the Bible is true." Yes, just act like the Bible's true! And, you know, just by my saying those words, that deacon board sighed a sigh of relief! Because they knew the Bible is true.

If you know God's Word is true and you act like it is true, the Bible will become real in your life. You will bring God on the scene in your life!

In families, different troublesome issues arise. And sometimes among relatives, difficult problems arise also. (I'm not talking here about my immediate family, because we taught our children to act upon God's Word, and they did.)

Sometimes the problems and circumstances which arise in a church seem difficult too. And sometimes Christians (and even Spirit-filled Christians) seemed to be overwhelmed by these problems, and would say to me, "What are we going to do now?" I would smile and say, "I don't know what *you* are going to do, but I'll tell you what *I'm* going to do. I'm just going to act like the Bible is true."

I remember one particular occasion along this line which occurred just after my oldest brother had gotten saved. (He had gotten saved because I had acted on God's Word, broken the power of the devil over his life, and claimed his salvation.) He was only a few weeks old in the Lord, when this incident took place.

I took care of my mother's business affairs for her, and although I really needed to attend to something for her,

I was unable to because I was in a revival in Dallas with two services a day. My brother Dub said he wanted to see our grandfather anyway, who was 90 years old and about ready to pass over to the other side, so Dub said he would go see the relatives and take care of this matter for me.

Taking care of this business involved dealing with some difficult relatives. When my brother Dub returned after visiting them, he said, "Boy, I'll tell you, I just about got whipped." One of the relatives had gotten rough with him.

My brother continued, "I told this relative, 'If you know God or have any knowledge of God you'd better thank Him I'm not like I used to be, or I would have whipped you already.'" (He was telling the truth; he would have!)

My brother said to this relative, "I'm saved now and I've quit fighting. I'm not going to fight you, but if you get on me, I'm going to get you off me. And you'd better just pray you don't get hurt if I have to get you off me!" Well, this relative didn't fight Dub, but he did give him a good "cussing out."

Putting the Lord To Work for You

I said to my brother, "Dub, I'll go up there and finish taking care of this matter. Your trouble is, you're just a new Christian and you don't know how to put the Lord to work for you."

Through the years, I've had the greatest time in the world putting the Lord to work for me — just letting Him and His Word do the work. There is a Scripture which says, *"the battle is the Lord's"* (1 Sam. 17:47). I let Him fight all my battles. I don't fight any. The battle is the Lord's,

but the victory is ours. Second Chronicles 20:15 says, "...
*Be not afraid nor dismayed ... for the battle is not yours,
but God's.*" When I put God's Word to work for me, the
Word fights my battles for me.

So I have never been in a battle and I have been saved
more than 50 years. Since I learned about faith and that
the Bible says, "*For we which have believed do enter into
rest ...*" (Heb. 4:3), I've been in a state of rest.

Grasp what this Scripture says: "*we which have
believed do enter into rest.*" Notice it does not say we have
entered into a state of fear or into a state of fretting, grip-
ing, worrying, or fighting. No! It says we have entered
into *rest.*

Walking in Victory

For more than 50 years I have been in a state of rest.
I haven't had any battles. I have simply put God's Word
to work for me. Some people battle themselves to death;
they're always in some kind of a battle.

"How goes the battle?" some ask. I always answer,
"The victory is wonderful!" Hallelujah! There isn't any
battle; I'm enjoying the victory. Faith always has a good
report!

Back again to what I was saying to my brother Dub.
I told him, "You just don't know how to put the Lord to
work for you. You see, the Bible says in First John 4:4,
'*... greater is he that is in you, than he that is in the world.*'
Now, Dub, I'm going to act like that Scripture is true. I
want to show you how to practice the Word — how to put
the Word to work for you."

I continued, "When the Bible says that greater is He

that is in you than he that is in the world, the 'He' that
is in you is God, the Holy Spirit. And the 'he' that is in
the world is the devil himself, who is the god of this world.
(Second Corinthians 4:4 calls him the god of this world.)

"I believe that the God who is in me is bigger than the
devil. Do you believe that? I believe that the Holy Spirit
who is in me is greater than the devil who is in the world
— just as the Word of God says."

To get the full impact of this truth, let's look at the
following verses in First John:

> 1 JOHN 4:1-4
> 1   Beloved, believe not every spirit, but try the spirits
> whether they are of God: because many false prophets are
> gone out into the world.
> 2   Hereby know ye the Spirit of God: Every spirit that con-
> fesseth that Jesus Christ is come in the flesh is of God:
> 3   And every spirit that confesseth not that Jesus Christ
> is come in the flesh is not of God: and this is that spirit
> of antichrist, whereof ye have heard that it should come;
> and even now already is it in the world.
> 4   Ye are of God, little children, and have overcome them:
> because greater is he that is in you, than he that is in the
> world.

The Battle Has Been Won

In the first three verses, John, talking about evil spirits
and demons, said, *"Ye have overcome them."* Notice that
he did not say that you are *going to* overcome these evil
spirits and demons. He said that you *have* overcome them.
In other words, the victory over evil spirits, demons, and
every power that is in this world has already been
accomplished for you. The battle has already been fought,
and the battle has already been won! You don't have to

fight the battle, because the battle has already been won!

Then John qualifies this statement that the believer has overcome every demon and every evil spirit. These Scriptures tell us exactly how it is that the believer has overcome them. It is because, ". . . *greater is he that is in you, than he that is in the world.*"

Colossians 1:27 says, ". . . *Christ in you, the hope of glory.*" You see, by the power of the Holy Spirit, Christ is dwelling in you. Jesus has already defeated all demons, and all evil spirits. Everything Jesus did, He did as your substitute. Everything Jesus did is marked down by God *to your credit!*

Let that soak in. Can you understand that? That's the way God looks at Jesus' victory. And really, that's the way the devil looks at it too. Satan knows that you have overcome him through Jesus' victory. But as long as you don't know it, he takes advantage of you.

The Greater One

So I said to Dub, "Greater is He that is in me than he that is in the world. The God who is in me, the Jesus who is in me, the Spirit of God who is in me — is greater than the spirit of the devil who is in those relatives. Because the love of God has been shed abroad in my heart by the Holy Spirit (Rom. 5:5), the love that is in me, is greater than the hate that is in them."

Here was my grandfather, 90 years old and about to die, and some of the relatives were already fussing about who was going to get what. Unsaved people will do that because they are selfish.

I decided to leave after my morning service and drive

the 30 miles from Dallas to attend to this family business myself. Before I left, Momma said, "Son, don't get into any trouble. I'm not concerned about getting anything. I am only concerned about him (my grandfather — her father) and about his comfort. Don't get into it with the relatives and get into trouble."

"Momma, I'm not going to have any trouble."

"Well," she said, "So-and-so almost whipped Dub."

"I'm not Dub, and they are not about to whip me. The God who is in me is bigger than the devil who is in them."

I said, "I won't have any trouble. I'll never have any trouble."

When I arrived, I parked my car in my grandfather's driveway. The man who had caused so much trouble with Dub lived next door. When his wife saw my car, she called me over to the back porch.

Then she began, "I'll tell you, Ken . . . I'll tell you . . ." And the more she talked, the more she ranted and raved. And you know, I felt so sorry for her.

A Child of the Devil

I thought, *Dear Lord, dear Lord. Here is this poor old soul, she can't help but have the nature of the devil in her because she's a child of the devil; full of hate and selfishness, worried about what she is going to get and whether someone is going to get more than she is of the property.*

I felt so sorry for her. She couldn't help being that way. She couldn't help having the nature of the devil in her, because she was a child of the devil.

I didn't say a word to her. I simply said to the Lord

in my heart, "Thank God, the Greater One is in me." I just acted like the Greater One was in me. And He is greater. He's greater than the devil in her. The love of God that is in me is greater than the hatred in her. As I said, I felt so sorry for her.

Although she was looking down as she grew louder with her ranting and raving and plain old Texas cussing, she suddenly looked up at me. I guess such a look of love and compassion must have come over my face that when she looked up, she just sputtered to a close. Nothing else came out of her mouth.

Then she reached up, took ahold of my hand, got down on her knees, and cried, "My God, put your hands on my head and pray for me. A poor old soul like me needs something. Oh, my God, pray for me!"

Until then I hadn't said a word. All I had done was to act like the Bible is true. And it *is* true, praise God! Greater is He who is in me than he that is in the world.

She said, "We don't want to be cheated out of anything, but now we don't want your momma to be cheated out of anything either."

'Inside Information'

"Don't you worry about Momma," I said. "She'll get everything that is coming to her, because, you see, I have some 'inside information.' "

"Oh," she said, "you do?"

"Yes, I do," I didn't tell her what 'inside' information it was. I didn't tell her it was information *inside* the Bible and *inside* me.

She called her husband home from work. He was so

apologetic, and only the day before he had been cussing and raising the devil. He said, "Well now, we're not so concerned about ourselves . . ."

I knew he was lying, because I knew they were going to instigate a suit as soon as my grandfather died to try to get all of his property.

He continued, "When my wife called me, she said you had some 'inside information.'"

"I surely do. I do have some 'inside information.'"

He changed his attitude. He said, "I'll tell you one thing, we're going to see that your momma gets her share."

"I'm sure of that," I said.

And sure enough, they did. Momma got her share, praise God.

I believe the Greater One lives in us. I believe He is greater than the devil. I know the Word of God says that, so I must act like it is true. When I begin to act like the Word of God is true, that's when it becomes a *reality* in my life. That is when the Greater One goes to work for me.

If I act like *I* must fight the battle, He can't fight it. If I fight the battle, I am not taking advantage of the Greater One and what He has done for me. Can you see that? So I don't try to figure out the situation. I just lie down and go to sleep and let the Greater One fight my battles for me, praise God. I don't care what's going on, that's the attitude I take.

Troubled Churches

In the years I pastored, almost every church God sent me to was a church that had trouble. Concerning one church in particular, I guess it's a good thing I hadn't known all the "ins and outs" about it before I accepted the pastorate. I didn't apply for the pastorate. I had held a meeting there and the board contacted me, told me their pastor was leaving, and asked me if I would take the church. God had already dealt with me before they contacted me, so I accepted.

I found out later that nobody else would have it. But after we pastored that church, God blessed and it came out well. When I left, 40 preachers applied for the pastorate of that church.

But you know, while I was pastoring that church I didn't have any trouble. Sometimes if problems would arise, I would say to the people, "I'm not going to bother about these problems. They are not going to bother me one bit." I meant that I wasn't going to bother about these petty problems, even if the deacons decided to have a fist fight in the churchyard. I would have let them go ahead and fight. I wouldn't even have gone out to try to stop them. When they got it all fought out I would have gone out, prayed with them, and gotten them back in fellowship so we could go on with God.

Casting Cares on Him

First Peter 5:7 says, "*Casting all your care upon him, for he careth for you.*" Let's look at that in *The Amplified Bible:*

1 PETER 5:7
7 Casting the whole of your care — all your anxieties, all your worries, all your concerns, once and for all — on Him; for He cares for you affectionately, and cares about you watchfully.

I have done that. God has my cares. He's figured them all out and He is working on them, and I'm shouting while He's doing it! God is doing the work, and I am doing the shouting. Praise the Lord!

You see, if you are lying awake at night trying to figure out the situation for God, trying to work out how He can solve your problems, then He doesn't have your burdens; you still have them.

The faith life is the most beautiful life in the world, and it is the life God wants us to live. "*. . . The just shall live by faith"* (Rom. 1:17). And the walk God wants us to walk is the faith walk. *"For we walk by faith, not by sight"* (2 Cor. 5:7).

It's those who *act* upon God's Word who get results. You act faith. You talk faith. Your actions and your words must agree that you are a *believer.* It will not do you any good to *talk* faith if you are not going to *act* faith. And if it were somehow possible for you to act faith without talking faith, that would not do you any good either. Let both your words and your actions agree.

Some people will say one moment, "I'm trusting God to meet my needs." But with the very next breath they say, "Well, it looks like I'm going to lose my car. I can't make my payments." One minute it sounds like they are talking faith, but within a short time their actions prove they are not.

Some will even quote God's Word and say, "I know the Lord said in Philippians 4:19, *'But my God shall supply all your need according to his riches in glory by Christ Jesus.'* I'm trusting the Lord to meet all our needs, but it looks like we will have to have the telephone taken out. We can't pay the bill."

You see, it sounded in the beginning as if they were talking faith. They even quoted Scripture. But this was not really faith speaking. Really, they just mentally assented that this verse is in the Bible. They mentally agreed to its truth, but they didn't act as if it were so. In order to get results you must start acting like God's Word is true!

Jeremiah 1:12 says, "*. . . I will hasten my word to perform it.*" The margin of my *King James* translation says, "I will watch over my word to perform it." Well, you may be certain that if you accept God's Word and act on it, He is watching over that Word to make it good in your life!

Acting on the Word

All you need to do is to *act on the Word.* It's deeply important that you learn this simple little lesson, because it is not struggling, it is not crying, it is not fretting, it is *acting* on what God has spoken that brings results!

More than 40 years ago I was holding a meeting in a Full Gospel church in West Texas. I didn't know as much then as I know now, but, on the other hand, I knew more than what I was acting on in this particular instance.

If you are associating with people (even Christians) who are full of doubt and unbelief, it is easy for some of that to rub off on you. And if you're not careful, you will unconsciously pick up some of their statements and attitudes.

The pastor of this Full Gospel church knocked on my bedroom door one morning and handed me an air mail special delivery letter which my wife had mailed the night before. My wife wrote me that both of our children were sick. She had been up with them day and night for several days, and she was worn out and desperate. Then, too, we were in desperate financial straits.

It just so happened that the day I received the letter from my wife was the regular visitation day for the pastor of this church where I was preaching. The pastor and his wife would be spending the entire day visiting different members of their congregation. This meant I would have the whole day to myself. After they left, I got my Bible and that letter and went over to the church. I knelt down before the altar, opened up that letter, and read it to the Lord.

Struggling in Prayer

"Now, Lord," I said, "my babies are sick. My poor, dear little wife has been up with them day and night until she is worn out physically. She needs help and rest. Then we are in dire need financially. Now I've come out here, and I'm going to stay out here all day if necessary." (See, I was making quite a struggle out of it.)

"I'm going to pray," I told God, "until I pray through and those babies are healed and these financial needs are met."

Well, I prayed, and I prayed, and I prayed. But it seemed as if the longer I prayed, the further away from the answer I got, and the worse I felt.

I prayed around the altar on my knees. I prayed walking up and down the aisles of that church. I spent about an hour and a half praying, walking, beating the altar, kicking my feet, and doing everything else I had ever seen Full Gospel people do.

I thought, *Well, if it worked for them, it will work for me.* But the only results after an hour and a half were that I had used up so much physical energy, I had pretty well worn myself out.

I decided to give it up as a bad job, and went back to the parsonage for a drink of water. But as I sat there and thought about my family, I said, "Well, bless God, I'm not going to be so easily defeated." So I got up and went back to the church.

Kneeling before the altar again, I opened that letter, read it to the Lord, and said, "Now, Lord, I'm determined this time to stay here all day if necessary. I'm going to stay here until I pray through; until I know those children are healed and the financial needs are met."

So I went at it again. And after another hour and a half, I had worn myself out again. Then the third time, I went through the entire process again.

Finally, after almost four hours, I lay down on the wide altar, exhausted. My hands were folded beneath my head and I was staring at the ceiling. But I had gotten quiet.

Hearing From God

In the Old Testament there is a Scripture that says, *"Be still, and know that I am God..."* (Ps. 46:10). Many times we cannot hear what God is trying to say to us on the inside because we don't get quiet before Him. You can be as noisy with your mind as you can be with your hands and feet. It is pretty easy to quiet your body down to be still, but it is sometimes difficult to keep your mind from thinking. Have you ever had "head" trouble? "Head" trouble is when you have been able to quiet your body, but your mind just keeps on going. Sometimes when you get down to pray that happens.

Lying there on the altar, I was finally quiet. My body was quiet, and my mind was quiet. I am convinced that the Spirit of God had been trying to arrest my attention all that time to get something over to me. But for almost four hours I had been making so much noise I couldn't hear Him! Some people never do hear from God, because they are too busy with their own thoughts and their own physical efforts.

When I did get quiet, inside me I heard these words: "What are you doing out here acting like this?" (I realized it was the "still small voice" of the Holy Spirit speaking plainly to me.)

I felt insulted! Rising up to a seated position, I grabbed that letter, and began to wave it and to say, "Now Lord, I've read this letter to You three times. Don't You understand? My babies are sick and my dear little wife has been up with them day and night for two or three days. She's worn to a frazzle. We are in dire need financially. And You ask me why I am out here acting like this?" I thought that got it told! (But it didn't.)

I lay back down on the altar, thinking that should settle it, and I got quiet again. Then on the inside of me I heard, "What are you doing out here acting like this?"

I rose up again, grabbed the letter, and said, "Lord, I've already told You! I read the letter to You three times and told You what it said. I'm not going to read it any more. Don't You understand? My babies are sick. My dear little wife is there by herself. She's been up day and night caring for them till she's worn out. We are in dire financial need. And You ask what I am doing out here?"

I thought surely that should be enough for Him to understand, and I lay back down on the altar and got quiet again.

Then the third time, on the inside of me, I heard these words, "What are you doing out here acting like this?"

This time I got up off the altar and stood by it, waving the letter before Him. "Lord, I've read You this letter three times. This is the third time I will have told You what it says. Don't You understand? My babies are sick and my dear little wife is at home with them by herself. She's been up with them night and day until she's worn herself out. We have financial needs." And then I stopped.

When I did, inside of me I heard these words: "Well, what did you come out here for?"

What's 'Praying Through'?

"Lord, I came out here to pray through."

"What do you mean by 'pray through'?"

"Well," I said, "uh, er, uh, well, uh, well, er, uh . . ." As I began to think about it, I realized I didn't know what I meant. So I said, "Whatever it is those Full Gospel people mean by it, *that's* what I've come out here to do. I've heard them say it."

As I thought about it, I said to Him, "Now I guess what I thought was that I was going to pray until I had some kind of feeling or witness or something like that. You see, I'm 365 miles away from home and I'd like to have some kind of witness or something; some kind of feeling that this prayer is being answered. I don't know what I meant, but I think that I thought I would know in some way or another when this prayer was answered — when

the children were healed and when our needs were met."
He said, "Isn't My Word sufficient for you?"

"Oh, yes, Lord. You know there isn't anyone in the
whole state of Texas who believes Your Word any more
than I do. There isn't anyone in the United States — (Then
I got really bold.) — there isn't anyone in the world, who
believes Your Word any more than I do. You know that
I have always been a stickler for Your Word."

"Well," He said, "you are not acting like My Word is
so. In fact, you are acting as though My Word were not
so. You are acting like you have to talk Me into the idea
of doing what I said I would do in My Word. You are
acting as though you think that if you pray long enough
and loudly enough you might eventually talk Me into the
notion of not being a liar, and keeping My Word."

His Word Is Sufficient

And then I saw it! I cried, "Dear God, forgive me. I
have been running with unbelieving Christians so long it
has rubbed off on me. I've picked up some of their habits
and some of their speech. Forgive me. No, I don't need
to 'pray through.' I don't need to have any kind of feeling. I don't need any kind of witness. Your Word *is* sufficient for me! That's all I need — just Your Word."

Then He spoke to me on the inside, "Doesn't My Word
say *I* took your children's infirmities and *I* bare their sicknesses?"

I knew He was quoting Matthew 8:17 to me, which
says, "*. . . Himself took our infirmities, and bare our sicknesses.*" And you see, if He took our infirmities and bare
our sicknesses, then health and healing belong to us and

to our children too. So He put it that way: "Doesn't My Word say that I took your children's infirmities and I bare their sicknesses?"

"It surely does," I said.

"Isn't that all the evidence you need?" He asked.

"It surely is. That's all I need. I want to thank You right now for answering my prayer."

Acting on the Word

As soon as I said that — I was acting on God's Word! Even though I was praying before, I wasn't acting on God's Word. I was in unbelief. It's not struggling, laboring, and *trying to believe* that brings results. It's acting on God's Word that brings results.

I said to Him, "Your Word is all the evidence I need, Lord. I want to thank You right now because my babies are both well. By Your Word they are healed. Praise the Lord! Hallelujah! Thank You for it now."

Immediately something said to my mind (I recognized it to be the devil.), "Now how can you tell whether or not they are well when you are 365 miles away?"

I said, "Because the Word says, 'Himself took my children's infirmities and bare their sicknesses.' Therefore, my children are well."

Then I asked the Lord about our financial need. He said, "Didn't I say in Philippians 4:19, *'But my God shall supply all your need according to his riches in glory by Christ Jesus'?*"

"You said it, Lord," I replied, "and Your Word is all the evidence I need. Thank You for it. Thank You our needs are met. Praise God! Hallelujah!"

The Burden Lifts

The burden was gone. I picked up my Bible, picked up the letter, and went out the door whistling and singing. I tell you, the grass was greener, the flowers were prettier, the sun was brighter, and everything was lovely.

The next morning another air mail special delivery letter arrived from my wife. "Everything is fine," she wrote. She was feeling well and strengthened. Then she told me that the previous morning both of the children — just as if you had snapped your fingers — were instantly well. Both of them! Instantly! The sickness didn't gradually go away, as sometimes happens. They were instantly well! Glory to God! And the finances had been met too. Praise the Lord!

Too often we want to put ourselves into the battle rather than letting God fight for us. We want to help Him. We want to figure out how God can fight our battle. We keep struggling and struggling and struggling — and the job never gets done because we won't turn it over to Him. God would fight every battle for us if we would let Him.

A Nagging Wife Reforms

One lady said to me, "Brother Hagin, I can see it now: I can see how to let God fight my battles for me. I was overly concerned about my husband. He was lost. I kept nagging at him about going to church, but he wouldn't go. Once in a while, if I would nag long enough, he might go on a Sunday night.

"Then I saw that I was trying to save him myself. When I realized this, I simply said to the Lord, 'Lord, I'm just going to act on Your Word and claim his salvation and forget it. I'm not even going to pray for him anymore.' I just quit all that nagging and for about three months I didn't even invite him to go to church. Every time I thought about his salvation I would say, 'Thank God I have turned his salvation over to the Lord. The Lord is working it out.'

"In those three months I did not say one word to my husband about God, the church, or about anything spiritual. Then one Sunday morning as he sat at the breakfast table reading the paper, I noticed he was looking around that paper at me as I cleared the table and got him another cup of coffee. Finally, he asked, 'Aren't you going to ask me to go to church this morning?'

"I told him that I wasn't going to ask him to go to church at all anymore, and he asked me why I wasn't. So I said to him, 'It may be of interest to you to know that I am not fooling with you anymore about spiritual things. In fact, I'm not even praying for you anymore.'

" 'You're not?' he exclaimed. 'Don't quit praying for me!' "

She didn't tell him that she had turned it over to the Lord and claimed his salvation. She just said to him, "I'm not even praying for you anymore." Then she went on and started getting ready for church. When she was ready and came out to go to church, there was her husband, ready to go too.

"Maybe I'll go with you this morning," he said.

"It's entirely up to you," she said, acting as if she didn't care whether he went or not.

But he went. And he went the next Sunday, and the next Sunday. On the third Sunday he was saved!

'Helping God'

The Lord does use people to carry out His will on the earth, but sometimes, without any leading of the Lord, we try to do His work for Him. We do this because we are concerned, and we should be concerned. But there is a fine line here; we need to differentiate between helping Him and getting in His way.

In praying for my own relatives, I didn't realize where I was missing it until the Lord showed me. When you bring requests to the Lord *and* act on His Word, you get results.

For example, I prayed for my oldest brother for more than 15 years. Several times I fasted. But the more I fasted and prayed, the worse he got. If my prayers ever made any impression on him, I don't know it. And finally, after 15 years, I was almost ready to give up. But then I began to see what the Bible says.

Prayer is right and fasting is right, but I saw one day why my prayer and fasting wasn't working: It was because I wasn't really trusting God to do the work in my brother's life. I was trying to do it myself. It was all labor with me; it was all works. It was as if I were trying to force God into doing something.

I was doing the same thing with Dub that I'd done the day God spoke to me in that church, and said: "You are acting like My Word isn't so. You are acting as if you have to talk Me into the idea of doing what I have already promised to do."

I saw this in regard to my brother. And I also saw this: As believers, we have authority and we have power. So one day I took my authority as a believer. I stood there in my bedroom and said, "I take the Name of Jesus and break the power of the devil over Dub's life and claim his deliverance from the devil and claim his salvation." I picked up my Bible and went out of the room singing and whistling. "Well, that's it," I said. "It is done. Praise God!"

I was acting on God's Word. I didn't think about it or pray about Dub's salvation again. Once I settle a case in victory, I don't think about it anymore. However, twice in the next week, just as plainly as some person speaking to me, a voice came against my mind saying, "Oh, come on now. You don't really think old Dub will ever be saved, do you?"

Staying in Faith

I had been walking across the room and I stopped. I started to think about it in my mind a little, but I recognized what I was doing, and that it was Satan talking to my mind, so I shut my mind off. If Satan can hold you *in the arena of reason in your mind,* he will defeat you every time. But if you hold him in the *arena of faith,* you will defeat him every time.

I began to laugh on the inside of me, right out of my spirit, and said, "No, I don't *think* he'll be saved. I *know* he'll be saved! Because you see, devil, I have taken the Name of Jesus and broken your power over Dub."

Twice the devil asked me that question and twice I told him the same thing. Within ten days, Dub was saved.

Someone asked me, "What if it hadn't worked that fast?" It wouldn't have bothered me at all. I would have held fast to God's Word and acted on it. If it had taken a hundred years, I would have known Dub would have been saved.

Smith Wigglesworth said that when you believe God — sometimes God will permit you to be tested right down to the last moment — but He still watches over His Word to perform it.

All you have to do is simply ask yourself the question, "Did God promise it in His Word?"

Is His Word true? Yes, it is, isn't it? Then act like it is and His Word will become real to you!

Chapter 6
Understanding Our Confession

Fight the good fight of faith....
— 1 Timothy 6:12

Sometimes people have said after having a little battle in the area of faith or a little fight in obtaining healing, "If I had just been there when Jesus was on the earth, getting healed would have been easy." However, if you go back and read the four Gospels, you will find that it was not so easy.

Take for instance, the woman with the issue of blood. Jesus said to her, "... *Daughter, thy faith hath made thee whole* ..." (Mark 5:34). It was not Jesus' faith, or someone else's faith, but it was *her* own faith that made her whole.

To receive her healing, this woman had a number of obstacles to overcome. You know yourself, it's not always the easiest thing in the world to overcome obstacles. First, according to the Book of Leviticus, a woman with an issue of blood was in the same category that a leper was in. She was not supposed to be in public, mixing and mingling with other people. If anyone came close to her she was to cry out, "Unclean! Unclean!" That was her religious teaching.

But this woman got right into that crowd, mixed and mingled with them, and reached right through all those people and touched Jesus' clothes. So she had this obstacle of "church" teaching to overcome in order to receive healing. But she overcame it.

Second, women in that country, especially in that day, did not have the rights and privileges of mixing freely in public which they have in most parts of the world today.

This woman had to overcome this obstacle too. She didn't pray that God would *remove* every obstacle; she just walked *over* every obstacle. *She* did something about those obstacles herself with her own faith. She got right into the midst of that crowd. And, of course, when she got to where Jesus was, the obstacle of the multitude thronging Jesus was there.

You could say, then, that the multitude stood between her and healing. Public sentiment stood between her and healing. Some of her own "church" teaching stood between her and getting to Jesus to be healed. But she did not pray that God would overcome these obstacles or remove them for her. She did something about these obstacles herself. With her faith, she persevered through every obstacle.

You, too, will have to do something about the obstacles which confront you and stand in your way of receiving healing. I have heard people actually pray, "Lord, make it easy for me to receive my blessing" — and yet not receive from God. You see, God puts all answers to prayer on a faith proposition. Too many people want God to do it all, leaving nothing for them to do and no part for them to play in receiving from Him. But we do have a part to play in receiving *answered prayer* from God.

And we will have obstacles to overcome just like the woman with the issue of blood did. *We* have *our part* to play because our text says that *we* are to, *"Fight the good fight of faith."* If there were no hindrances or enemies to faith, there would be no fight to faith.

The Bible tells us, *". . . faith cometh by hearing, and hearing by the Word of God"* (Rom. 10:17). Therefore, the greatest hindrance there is to faith is a lack of knowledge of God's Word. It is a mistake to pray for faith when what is really needed is a knowledge of God's Word. If you gain knowledge of God's Word, you will have faith. Faith comes by hearing, and hearing by the Word of God.

Faith will grow as our knowledge of God's Word grows. If faith is not growing, our knowledge of God's Word is not growing. I would be concerned if I did not have a *growing* faith.

It is a tragedy that people can believe God more when they are baby Christians than they can after they have been Christians for years. Instead of growing in faith, it seems as though some Christians deteriorate in faith. This should not be.

Why Many Fail

We have been looking at six hindrances to faith. Of course, all of these hindrances are related to a lack of knowledge of God's Word. The sixth hindrance to faith we shall look at is the reason many fail in receiving from God. Many fail because they do not understand what the Bible says about "confession."

When we use the word "confession," people instinctively think of confessing sin or confessing failure. And the Bible does say, *"If we confess our sins, he is faithful and just to forgive us our sins, and to cleanse us from all unrighteousness"* (1 John 1:9). But that is the negative side of confession. The Bible has *much more* to say about the positive side of confession, that is, about confessing our faith.

For example, confessing Jesus as Lord is the positive side of confession.

ROMANS 10:9
9   That if thou shalt confess with thy mouth the Lord
Jesus [Jesus is Lord], and shalt believe in thine heart that
God hath raised him from the dead, thou shalt be saved.

This confession does not refer to confessing sin. This
is confessing Jesus. It is not a negative confession, it is
a positive confession of faith.

Now notice another confession found in the next verse:

ROMANS 10:10
10 For with the heart man believeth unto righteousness;
and with the mouth confession is made unto salvation.

This, also, is not a negative confession. It is a positive
confession. "*. . . with the mouth confession is made unto
salvation.*" In other words, we could say that with the
mouth man confesses that he is saved.

Salvation Demands Confession

Did you know that no man is ever saved until he *confesses* that he is saved? I don't care if he feels saved —
he is still not saved until he confesses that he is saved.
God's Word says, "*. . . with the mouth confession is made
unto salvation.*" If Christians could ever fully grasp this
important truth: *The Bible says* it's with the *mouth* that
confession is made unto salvation! So our faith keeps pace
with our confession. Faith never rises above *our own confession.*

In a certain Full Gospel church in one of our large cities,
the men of the church were in the habit of coming to the
church each day for an early morning prayer meeting. An

unsaved man had been coming to these prayer meetings each morning for six months but had not yet received salvation.

When I came to this church to hold a meeting, one of the men there told me about this unsaved man. "Brother Hagin, I believe you can help him," this Christian man said. I knew I could, because God's Word will always straighten out anyone who will listen to it.

The men who attended these early morning prayer meetings worked during the week and they could not attend the morning teaching sessions we held during the meeting. So they asked me to teach at a Saturday night session for men only. This unsaved man came to the first Saturday night meeting with his Bible under his arm. We were introduced to each other, but we didn't have time to talk before the service began.

People were still coming in to the church, even though it was time to start, so I said, "While others are still coming, we'll have a few testimonies." One or two men testified and then I looked over at this unsaved man and said to him, "Get up and *confess* that you are saved."

That startled him. He said, "Oh! I'm not saved yet."

"I know it," I said, "but you see the Bible says that with the mouth confession is made unto salvation. You will never be saved until you confess you are and make a public statement of it, because Jesus said, '*Whosoever therefore shall confess me before men, him will I confess also before my Father which is in heaven*' " (Matt. 10:32).

"Yes," he said, "but I don't feel like I'm saved."

"Certainly not. You can't feel something you haven't got. You don't feel saved because you are not saved. You won't feel saved until you are saved, and you won't be saved until you confess it."

"Well, I — I," he stuttered, "I don't much believe I want to do that."

"I want to ask you a question," I said. "Is it correct that you have been coming here for six months, praying and repenting?"

"Oh, yes," he replied, "God knows I have prayed and repented every morning."

"Well, repentance has its place, but you have already done that, and you don't need to keep doing it again and again. Now you are ready for the next step. You see, if there were three steps into this building, just because you took the first step, or even the second, it would not mean you were in the building yet. If there are three steps to take to get into the building, you must take all three before you are inside the building."

(Some people will just take a step or two — and although the steps they take are Bible steps, they don't arrive with the answer because they don't take *all* the steps that lead to the particular provision God has promised.)

Then I said to this man, "You have your Bible. Open it to Romans 10:9,10 and read it aloud."

He read, *"That if thou shalt* confess *with thy mouth the Lord Jesus, and shalt believe in thine heart that God hath raised him from the dead, thou shalt be saved. For with the heart man believeth unto righteousness; and with the mouth* confession *is made unto salvation."*

I said to him then, "Confess that you are saved."

"No, I don't much believe I want to do that."

(Now, I do things sometimes that startle even me. And in this instance I did one of those things. The Spirit of God came upon me to anoint me to do it. Even as I spoke the words, I found myself thinking, *Is that coming out of me?* My head had nothing in the world to do with it.)

Suddenly I found myself pointing my finger at him, and with authority and sternness in my voice I said, "I command you! I command you to stand and confess you are saved!"

When I said that, he stood. He looked around about half scared and said, "Well, most of you know that I have been coming here for six months and praying every morning. And God knows I am tired of sin and that I have repented and repented, prayed and prayed, and cried and cried. The Bible does say right here, *'That if thou shalt confess with thy mouth the Lord Jesus, and shalt believe in thine heart that God hath raised him from the dead, thou shalt be saved.'*

"Well," he continued, "I believe that Jesus is the Son of God and that He died for my sins according to the Scriptures. And I believe that God raised Him from the dead for my justification. (He knew what the Bible said about it.) So I just confess Him as my Lord and Savior and confess that I am saved." Then he sat down so fast and hard, you would have thought he had knocked the bottom out of the seat.

To divert attention away from him, I quickly pointed to another fellow and said, "Brother, you stand and testify." He did. Then I pointed to another one and he testified too.

After these two had testified, I looked back at this fellow, and his face was lit up like a neon sign. I said to him, "Brother, you get up again now."

This time I didn't have to prod him. He jumped up as though that pew were wired with electricity. As he jumped off the seat he shouted, "Whoo! When I said that, something happened down here inside me."

I said, "Sure, something happened to you. It is with the mouth that confession is made, and when you made your confession, God imparted eternal life into your spirit. Praise God that's what happened!"

Two nights later he was filled with the Holy Spirit and began to speak with other tongues. The following summer, he and his family were on vacation and they stopped by where we were in a meeting.

In talking to us further, he said, "Brother Hagin, when I was trying to get saved, I would go to the church and pray and pray and I meant business. I was as honest and sincere as I could be. Every morning I would cry and repent and then every afternoon after work I would stop by the beer joint and drink with the fellows. But after I just simply made that confession, there was such a change in me. Instantly, I was even delivered from cigarettes. I had been carrying a pack of them in my pocket, and about a week later after breakfast I unconsciously reached for them. It was then that I realized I hadn't been smoking. My wife spoke up and said, 'I've been watching you and you haven't smoked a cigarette in a week.' "

He was a new man. And the inward man was dominating the outward man. Now some people don't have it that easy. That is because they allow the outward man to keep on dominating. They let the body dominate the man on the inside. However, if you will let that new man on the inside dominate, it is easy to keep the flesh under.

This man continued, "I didn't deliberately try to quit smoking. It was just that I was so carried away with the blessings of God and taken up with God that I didn't notice I hadn't smoked for a week. I threw that package away and cigarettes have never bothered me since then. And I went right past those beer joints too, and they were never any temptation to me again either."

Faith's Confession Creates Reality

When you make a positive confession of faith, it creates reality in your life. And then you walk in the reality of God's blessing.

Many people struggle because instead of being on the positive side of confession, they are on the negative side. Maintaining a positive confession is always such a battle with them: "Oh, I'm having such a time. Poor ole me."

Our faith keeps pace with our confession. Let me repeat: Our faith keeps pace with our confession. Faith never rises above its confession. As I said, I am not referring to the negative confession of sins, but to the positive confession of the Word of God and the positive confession of our faith in God's Word.

If we *confess* weakness, failure, and sickness — we destroy faith. If your need is healing, boldly make your confession that your diseases were laid on Jesus. Then hold fast to that confession. That is where the fight of faith comes in — in holding fast to our confession of faith. Hebrews 4:14 tells us to hold fast to our profession (or *confession*) of faith. When we hold fast to our confession, we bring God on the scene.

The reason that the majority of Christians though earnest, are weak, is because they have never really dared to confess what God's Word says about them. They have never dared confess *what* the Bible says they are — *who* the Bible says they are — or *what* the Bible says they *have*.

Our confessions rule us. That is a spiritual law which few of us realize. Jesus said, "*. . . whosoever shall say . . . and shall not doubt in his heart, but shall believe that those things which he saith shall come to pass; he shall have whatsoever he saith*" (Mark 11:23).

Notice that last phrase again, "*he shall have whatsoever he saith.*" What we say *is* our confession. What we *say* is our faith speaking — whether it is on the positive side or on the negative side. Jesus said that whosoever shall *say,* he shall have whatsoever he *saith*.

Did Jesus know what He was talking about, or are these just the words of an irresponsible dreamer? No, they are not the words of a dreamer! Jesus knew exactly what He was saying. What did Jesus say you shall have? He said you shall have "*what you say.*"

I tell people all the time, "If you are not satisfied with what you have in life, then change what you are saying. You have created what you have in your life with your own words."

So many people maintain a wrong confession instead of maintaining a right confession. A wrong confession is a confession of defeat, failure, and the supremacy of Satan.

Many people have more faith in the devil than they do in God. They don't mind at all talking about what the devil is doing and what he's going to do in their lives. They talk about Satan and his activities all the time. But try to get those same people to talk about what God is doing and what God will do in their lives, and they say, "Well, I would be afraid to talk about that!" Are they afraid God won't keep His Word? Are they afraid He is a liar? No, God will do everything He said He would do! Praise the

Lord! God will keep His Word!

All some people talk about is their combat with the devil and what a time they are having with Satan. They shouldn't have any trouble with the devil, because Jesus has already defeated the devil for them. If they knew the Word of God, they would know that Satan is already a defeated foe.

Colossians 2:15 says, *"And having spoiled principalities and powers, he made a shew of them openly, triumphing over them in it."* Jesus triumphed over them in His resurrection and put them to nought.

Therefore, always talking about your combat with the devil — how he is hindering you, how he is holding you in bondage, and how he is keeping you sick — is a confession of defeat. And as long as you talk that way defeat is what you are going to have.

Many times I have prayed for people who have been healed because of the "mass" or corporate faith present in a meeting, or because of my faith. All symptoms of their former diseases and sicknesses left. Yet, as they went their way, I had a heaviness in my spirit. I knew the same thing or something worse would come back on them. How did I know? Because the whine never left their voices so I knew they would go right back to whining and talking negatively, talking unbelief, and making negative confessions.

A wrong confession glorifies the devil. Talking about what a time you're having with the devil, what a battle you're having, how the devil is keeping you from success, how he is keeping you sick, how he is holding you in bondage, and all the things you are going through — these are all confessions that glorify the devil.

Don't Glorify the Devil

I know people wouldn't do it if they really knew what they were doing, but negative confessions and confessions that glorify what the devil is doing are an unconscious declaration that God, your Father, is a failure.

Most of the confessions and testimonies we hear from Christians, glorify the devil and what he is doing. You need to realize, too, that every time you testify, you are confessing *something*. You are either confessing to the supremacy of Satan, or to the supremacy of God. Too many times in church testimony meetings, Christians are unconsciously testifying to the supremacy of Satan by the way they talk.

When you testify and brag on Jesus, aren't you glorifying Jesus? When you tell what God has done and is doing, aren't you glorifying God? By the same token, if you get up and brag on the devil's works, you are glorifying the devil. Some Christians have glorified the devil more than they have glorified God. That is the reason they are in the mess they're in.

When you talk about the devil and what he has done, you are glorifying the devil and his works. When you talk about defeat, you are talking about the works of the devil. Defeat is not of God! God did not intend for the Church to be defeated, did He?

Let's look at what the Bible has to say about this. The Bible declares in Matthew 16:18 that the gates of hell shall not prevail against the Church. Paul, writing to the Church, said, "... *in all these things we are more than conquerors through him that loved us*" (Rom. 8:37). If he had just said we were conquerors, it would have been enough to make us a success. But, no, the Bible says that we are more than conquerors through Him!

All right, then, let's talk about what we are in Christ. Rather than saying, "Well, I'm just whipped! I'm defeated," get up and tell what the Bible says about you. Say, "I am a conqueror!"

"But it doesn't seem that I'm a conqueror," you may say. It may not seem that it is so, but your confession that you are a conqueror will create the reality of it in your life. Sooner or later you will become what you confess.

An evangelist told me about an incident that happened while he was holding a meeting in a Full Gospel church in a certain city. The wealthiest businessman in town was a member of this church. This man had a heart condition, and while the evangelist was in town, this businessman had a heart attack at home. His wife called the pastor and the evangelist to come and pray for him.

They went to the upstairs bedroom of this man's palatial home where he lay unconscious. The doctor said that he could not be moved even in order to take him to the hospital. The doctor told the man's wife that although they were giving him oxygen and doing all they could, he would never regain consciousness, but would die there in bed.

The evangelist and pastor laid hands on him and prayed, and as quickly as you could snap your fingers, this man opened his eyes and was all right!

He sat up, got out of bed, and walked downstairs to the living room, where he visited with the pastor and evangelist for about 45 minutes.

When the pastor and evangelist rose to leave, he did not go outside with them, as he was still wearing only pajamas and a robe and the weather was cold.

His wife, however, did follow them outside. She closed the door as she followed them so her husband could not hear her. Then she said to the evangelist, "Keep praying for him. Keep on praying for him."

The evangelist asked, "Why?"

"Well," she said, "the devil will come back and put that right back on him and he'll have another heart attack."

"Sister, you have more faith in the devil than you have in God! You've just stood right there and told me what the devil is going to do. You said, 'The devil is coming back and he's going to put that back on him. The devil is going to give him another heart attack.' Why don't you say instead, 'God has healed him. The devil is not going to put that back on him'?"

She answered, "Oh, I'd be afraid to say a thing like that."

"Why?" he asked.

Whispering, she replied, "Don't you know the devil would hear me?"

Many Christians are the same way, and some preachers are too. I was holding a meeting in the Los Angeles area one year when there was an epidemic of the Asian flu. Headlines of *The Los Angeles Times* said that 2 million people had Asian flu in the Los Angeles area alone.

In the suburb where we held the meeting, there were two high school football teams. The local paper reported that both of them cancelled their Friday night games due to the flu epidemic. One team had a squad of 39 men and not a single one came out for practice. The other squad had 41 men and only two showed up for practice. Our church building (which seated several hundred) had been full, but when this epidemic hit, so many people got the flu that the congregation was reduced to 40 people.

Someone asked me, "Aren't you afraid?"

I publicly declared, "This epidemic doesn't worry me. I will never have the Asian flu." And I never have.

When I have made confessions of faith such as that, I have had Full Gospel preachers say to me privately, "Aren't you afraid to make statements like that?"

I've answered, "No, why?"

They whispered, "Don't you know *the devil* will hear you?"

"Sure I know he will hear me. I said it for his benefit. He's the very one I want to hear me! There was no need for me to say it for God's benefit. God already knew it anyway. The devil is the one that I wanted to hear it."

Fear Opens the Door to the Devil

A number of years ago my wife and I went to visit someone we had heard was ill. "If you are afraid," this person cautioned, "you'd better not come in here. I've picked up a virus and I've got a bad case of it."

"Don't let it bother you a bit," I said. "I'll never have it."

But my wife said, "Well, maybe I'd better not go in. I might get it."

I told her to make her own choice. She did go ahead and go in with me, but sure enough she got sick just like she said she would. I did not get sick. I pointed that out to her and told her, "You *said* the wrong thing." She had spoken with a hesitancy. She had wavered. She came down with that illness almost before we got home. It jumped on her that fast.

If you open the door, the devil will accommodate you. Job said, *"For the thing which I greatly feared is come upon me, and that which I was afraid of is come unto me"* (Job 3:25). You open the door to the devil by being afraid. You open the door to the devil by saying the wrong thing and making the wrong confession.

Then there are also those who say, "I believe I'll just *try* that" only because they have heard someone teach on confession. Well, if you make confessions which are not really your own faith speaking, but are just spoken off the top of your head, so to speak — you will fall flat on your face and the devil will whip you badly.

It is only when you know what God's Word says for yourself and make your confessions of faith in line with God's Word that you cannot be defeated. That is why I encourage people to get into the Word for themselves. Find out what the Bible says about you as a Christian. Underline all the "in Him," "in Christ," "in whom," Scriptures and begin to confess them. Confess, "This is mine because I am in Christ. Because I am in Him, I have the provision of health, healing, prosperity, etc."

Find out what is yours. Find out what belongs to you in Christ. When you make your confession of faith because of what *you* see in God's Word, then, because you have the foundation of God's Word under you, you will never be defeated.

In the natural, when people maintain the wrong confession, naturally their confession of doubt, failure, and unbelief saps the very life out of them and destroys their faith. Their negative confession holds them in bondage.

But the confession of your faith which has grown out of knowledge of God's Word will defeat the devil in combat every time.

Peter wrote, "... *your adversary the devil, as a roaring lion, walketh about, seeking whom he may devour*" (1 Peter 5:8).

I think that is as far as some people read. They say, "Whoo, the devil is after me. It says here he is going about like a roaring lion. It seems like I can feel his hot breath on my neck right now. The devil's seeking whom he may devour, and I'm afraid he's about to devour me. You all pray for me that he won't get me." There really isn't any use to pray for people who talk like that, because the minute they started talking that way, the devil had them.

One preacher said to me, "Well, Brother Hagin, I've got the devil on the run!"

"Praise the Lord," I said.

"The trouble is," he said, "I'm running, and he's after me!"

But that's not what the Bible says! Certainly we have an enemy. This verse calls the devil, *"Your adversary."* An adversary is an opponent, an enemy; one who is arrayed against you; one who stands between you and victory, and between you and success.

"Your adversary the devil, as a roaring lion, walketh about [right down here on this earth because he is the god of this world], *seeking whom he may devour."*

If you stop reading right there, that's not a very pretty picture, is it? Yes, if you let him, the devil will try to scare you; and if you don't know the truth, you will get scared, because he walks about *as* a roaring lion. But we are not to stop reading there.

Peter is writing to Christians; he's not writing to sinners. The devil has already devoured the sinners and swallowed them up. He will swallow Christians up if they let him. Now what are we to do about it?

Are we just going to throw up our hands and say, "Well, there's nothing we can do. I'm so weak and unworthy. Poor ole me"? No! A thousand times no!

Are we just to roll over and play dead, saying "He'll go away if I pretend he's not there"? No! We're not to do that.

Resist the Devil

Well, what *are* we to do? Let's read on and do what the Scripture says to do. "*Whom resist stedfast in the faith* . . ." (1 Peter 5:9). I like one translation which says, "Whom resist steadfast in YOUR faith." In other words, you resist the devil by your faith in God's Word — your faith in what God said about the devil — your faith in what God said about you. You resist the devil with that! Hallelujah to Jesus!

James 4:7 puts it this way, "*Resist the devil, and he will flee from you.*" "You" is the understood subject of that sentence: "*YOU resist the devil. . . .*" It does not say to get someone else to resist him for you. We can help each other temporarily, but in the final analysis there are just some things you have to do for yourself.

James wrote this letter and this particular verse to the Church. But he did not write this letter in the following way: "Word has come to me that our beloved brother, the Apostle Paul, has had great success in casting out devils and in dealing with devils. I suggest you write to him and get him to do something about the devil for you." No, the Bible doesn't say that. You have just as much authority over the devil as the next person. *You* resist the devil and he will flee from *you.*

I looked up the word "flee" in several dictionaries. I wasn't satisfied with the different shades of definitions I could gather, until I got a dictionary about a foot thick which had more than one page on the word "flee." Under the heading "to flee" I found the definition I liked best. It defined "flee" as: "to flee from, to run from, as in terror."

At the time I was looking into the meaning of this word, a dam broke high up in the mountains bordering France and Switzerland. Billions of gallons of water came rushing down between those mountains and wiped out an entire town. One newspaper article read, "The townspeople are fleeing. . . ." These people were running from that deluge as in terror because their lives were in danger.

God's Word says, *"Resist the devil, and he will flee from you."* He will run *from you* as in terror!

Oh, he's not afraid of you as an individual. But when you find out what your rights and privileges are in Christ; when you find out the Name of Jesus belongs to you and that you have a *legal right* to the use of that Name; when he knows *you* have found out what that Name *will do —* then he will run from you as in terror!

Until then, he will hang around, and every chance he gets he will rub your nose in the dirt. He will keep you on the defensive and he will keep you defeated.

You resist the devil. *You* do something about him. God has already done all He is going to do about the devil. God sent Jesus, and Jesus arose victorious over the devil. Jesus defeated him for you, and now it is up to you to do something about him.

Believe and Confess

Find out what belongs to you and rise up and walk in the light of what is yours! The way these things become real to you is by believing them in your heart and confessing them with your mouth.

Romans 10:10 says, *"For with the heart man believeth unto righteousness; and with the mouth confession is made unto salvation."* That is not only true concerning salvation, it is true concerning everything you receive from God. Believing with the heart and confessing with the mouth *is the way you must receive from God.*

It is always with the heart that man believes, and with the mouth confession is made unto salvation, or the baptism of the Holy Spirit.

It is with the heart that man believes, and with the mouth confession is made unto healing.

It is with the heart that man believes, and with the mouth confession is made unto answered prayer. The Scriptures say this, and I have proved it many times over the years.

The Lord said to me years ago, "I want you to go teach My people faith. I have taught you faith through My Word, and I have permitted you to go through certain experiences. You have learned faith both through My Word and through experience. Now go teach My people faith. Teach them what I have taught you."

I heard a voice from heaven speak those words to me. So I just teach people what I have learned from the Word, and what I have learned from experience. And years ago as I was learning these truths, I put them to the test. God's Word stands the test!

If you really believe a thing in your heart and say it with your mouth, you will have it. Why? Because *Jesus* said you would in Mark 11:23. Some say, "I confessed something and I don't have it." I don't mind telling them, "Either you or Jesus is lying about it because Jesus said, '. . . *Whosoever shall say . . . and shall not doubt in his heart, but shall believe that those things which he saith shall come to pass; he shall have whatsoever he saith.*' "

Usually, though, if you let people talk long enough, they give themselves away. They'll say, "Brother Hagin, I want you to know I did exactly what this verse said and it just does not work."

"Well, if it doesn't work, then Jesus told a lie about it," I say to them.

They stop and say, "That's right, Jesus didn't lie, did He?"

"No."

Then they usually admit, "Well, I sort of wondered if it would work anyway."

You see, they were indefinite in their believing in the first place about whether or not it would work. To get confession to work for you, you are going to have to believe the Bible is so. Be specific in your believing. Find Scriptures that promise you what you need and confess the Word!

I remember I was holding a meeting in a Full Gospel church years ago. I was teaching from Mark 5, about the woman with the issue of blood, and that believing with the heart and confessing with the mouth is the way you receive from God. The woman with the issue of blood *said,*

"*. . . If I may touch but his clothes, I shall be whole*" (v. 28).

The pastor of this Full Gospel church said to me, "Brother Hagin, I trust that my brother-in-law will receive the baptism of the Holy Spirit while you are here. He has been seeking to be filled with the Spirit for 34 years. There's not a finer Christian in my church."

I didn't say anything to him, but I thought to myself, *I know he will receive.* I knew he would receive because God's Word works. God and His Word are one! God works through His Word and His Word is not bound. If you'll preach the Word of God, it will work!

So that night I preached along this line that you can have what you say. Some of those in the congregation were getting it, but it takes time for people to grab ahold of these things, especially if the congregation has never been trained in the principles of faith. You won't always be able to make some of these principles work in public meetings if the faith of the congregation isn't up to that level yet.

That was the case in this particular meeting. I did not try to minister to this man in public because I knew the faith of the congregation was not up to that level. Instead, I went back to the prayer room, to talk to this man individually because he came forward to receive the Holy Spirit.

I said to him, "If I understand correctly, you've been seeking the Holy Spirit for 34 years."

He said, "That's right, I sure have."

"Well," I said, "did you hear the text, Mark 11:23, where Jesus said, '*. . . he shall have whatsoever he saith.*'?"

He said, "That's right."

"Do you believe that?"

"Yes, it's all in there."

Then I asked him, "Will you do what I tell you to do?"

"I will if it's easy," he replied.

It seems everyone is looking for something easy! I told him, "It's the easiest thing you ever did in your life. Just stand right there and let's join hands and agree together as one. I am going to pray a prayer according to God's Word, and you pray it after me. But don't *just* say it. Don't just pray it out of your head — let your heart agree with it. Because, you see, the Bible says, '... *whosoever shall say ... and shall not doubt in his heart...*'" (Mark 11:23).

He said, "All right, I'll do it."

So I started praying and he followed me. I prayed, "Heavenly Father, I thank You because I have been born again, and I am Your child. I thank You because salvation is a gift. The Bible says, '*By grace are ye saved through faith*' (Eph. 2:8), and I have received salvation in faith. Now, Father, the Word of God also teaches that the Holy Spirit is a gift, and by faith I now receive the Holy Spirit. I believe in my heart, and because I believe in my heart I say with my mouth, 'I receive the Holy Spirit. I am filled with the Holy Spirit.'" He followed me in this prayer. Then I just quoted Acts 2:4, and he repeated it after me. "Father, Your Word says, '*And they were all filled with the Holy Ghost, and began to speak with other tongues, as the Spirit gave them utterance.*' I believe that in my heart." As he said this, he instantly began to talk in tongues. One simple little prayer of believing in the heart and confessing with the mouth, and this man was filled with the Spirit after seeking this experience for 34 years!

There was another man standing by watching us, and he said, "Brother Hagin, I'd like to try that." I said, "It won't work then. It won't work if you just *try* it. This man didn't try it, he did it!'' He said, "Well, I'll do it then.'' When he got to the same place in his confessing what he believed in his heart, he began to speak in tongues too. You see, he confessed with his mouth and believed with his heart that he received the Holy Spirit, and the Holy Spirit gave him utterance.

I tested things out purposely. For example, another time I was in a home meeting with some denominational people who didn't have the teaching Full Gospel people have along these lines. I wanted to put God's Word to work and prove this principle — that you can have what you say. So I did not tell these people or even suggest to them that when they received the Holy Spirit they were to talk in tongues.

Nine people wanted to receive the Holy Spirit that night. I simply sat down with them and said, "Let's see what the Bible says about receiving the Holy Spirit." We looked at Scriptures in the Book of Acts and then I had all of them pray a prayer after me. I never told them that they were going to talk in tongues. I didn't even mention tongues or that tongues was the Bible evidence of receiving the baptism of the Holy Spirit.

In unison they all prayed, "Father, because I believe it in my heart, and I say it with my mouth, I am now filled with the Holy Spirit." Eight out of the nine people instantly started talking in tongues. They weren't taught to; they had never heard anyone talk about tongues. They just obeyed the Word of God! It proved to me beyond all shadow of doubt that when you are filled with the Holy Spirit, you will speak with other tongues.

"With the mouth confession is made unto . . . ," and *"He shall have whatsoever he saith."* These phrases from

God's Word say the same thing using different words. You are not going to have victory by confessing defeat, are you?

"With the mouth confession is made unto...." *"He shall have whatsoever he saith."* If you believe it in your heart and say it with your mouth, you'll have it! You are not going to have health by confessing sickness, are you?

"With the mouth confession is made unto...." *"He shall have whatsoever he saith."* You are not going to have your needs met by confessing poverty, are you?

You are not going to have success by confessing defeat and failure, are you?

It is amazing the faith that people have in the wrong things. And because they believe in the wrong things, they constantly talk the wrong things. They *believe* in sickness, so they talk sickness. They *believe* in defeat, so they talk defeat.

I don't believe in sickness. I believe sickness exists, because you see it everywhere.

However, I *believe* in health, so I constantly *talk* healing and health.

At times when I've had symptoms of a cold, some have said to me, "Oh, you're getting a cold."

I say, "No, I don't have a cold and I'm not going to have one. The devil is trying to give me one, but I'm not going to receive it." Those symptoms leave me right then.

I am trying to teach you how to *practice* faith. Faith will work for you. We walk by faith and not by sight, God's Word declares. So go ahead and walk by faith. Quit walking by sight. Most people also talk by sight rather than *talking* by faith. But we are to talk by faith. Talk faith. Act faith. Let your words and your actions agree. That makes you a believer.

I do not believe in defeat, so I never talk defeat. I do not believe in failure, so I never talk failure. I do not believe God is sick, or that He is a failure, or that He is defeated. He has never been a failure or defeated and He never will be. So why should I believe in and talk defeat, failure, and sickness?

Confess Your Faith

I don't believe that Jesus is sick, do you? I don't believe that Jesus is defeated, do you? I don't believe that Jesus is a failure, do you? I believe Jesus is the Healer, and because He is the Healer, I have health. I believe that I am more than a conqueror through Him who loved me and gave Himself for me.

I believe if Christians will find out who they are and what they are in Christ, they will rise to the level of what belongs to them!

The trouble is, however, that some people are looking at things from the natural — from a *physical* standpoint. God is looking at things from a *spiritual* standpoint. But some Christians keep looking at themselves from the physical and they see this world of darkness and, consequently, they walk by sight and not by faith. They think defeat, they talk defeat, and then they are defeated! And they sing those old unbelieving songs such as, "Here I wander like a beggar through the heat and through the cold." These are the things that defeat Christians.

Find out what the Bible says and begin to confess, "This is what I am in God. This is who I am in Christ."

You see, I do not believe that Christ is sick. There should not be any sickness in His Body! I don't believe that Jesus is defeated or that He is a failure. I believe that He is a conqueror! And that is why the Bible says, *". . . we are more than conquerors through him that loved us"* (Rom. 8:37).